t.f.h

W9-DHU-464

The Proper Care of
FINCHES

PHILLIP ST. BLAZEY

A trio of male Zebra Finches.

Photography: Dr. Herbert R. Axelrod, Helmut Bechtel, Horst Bielfeld, Bird Depot Inc., Rebecca Brega, Joshua Charap, Michael DeFreitas, G. Dingerkus, Herschel Frey, Michael Gilroy, Ray Hanson, Paul Kwast, Harry V. Lacey, P. Leysen, Dan Martin, R. and V. Moat, A.J. Mobbs, Mervin F. Roberts, H. Schempf, Vincent Serbin, W.A. Starika, Tony Tilford, Vogelpark Walsrode.

Drawings: John R. Quinn, R.A. Vowles.

Distributed in the UNITED STATES to the Pet Trade by T.F.H. Publications, Inc., 1 TFH Plaza, Neptune City, NJ 07753; on the Internet at www.tfh.com; in CANADA by Rolf C. Hagen Inc., 3225 Sartelon St., Montreal, Quebec H4R 1E8; Pet Trade by H & L Pet Supplies Inc., 27 Kingston Crescent, Kitchener, Ontario N2B 2T6; in ENGLAND by T.F.H. Publica-tions, PO Box 74, Havant PO9 5TT; in AUSTRALIA AND THE SOUTH PACIFIC by T.F.H. (Australia), Pty. Ltd., Box 149, Brookvale 2100 N.S.W., Australia; in NEW ZEALAND by Brooklands Aquarium Ltd., 5 McGiven Drive, New Plymouth, RD1 New Zealand; in SOUTH AFRICA by Rolf C. Hagen S.A. (PTY.) LTD., P.O. Box 201199, Durban North 4016, South Africa; in JAPAN by T.F.H. Publications, Japan—Jiro Tsuda, 10-12-3 Ohjidai, Sakura, Chiba 285, Japan. Published by T.F.H. Publications, Inc.
MANUFACTURED IN THE
UNITED STATES OF AMERICA
BY T.F.H. PUBLICATIONS, INC.

Contents

Introduction 7

Accommodation 14

Stock Selection 40

Feeding 52

Breeding 73

Health Matters 104

Finch Species 117

Index 254

By the nineteenth century, the widespread popularity of cage birds resulted in public shows—depicted here is the 1865 exhibition held in the Crystal Palace, London.

Introduction

Aviculture, the keeping of birds in captivity, has been a popular pursuit of mankind for over 2,000 years. Certainly Alexander the Great sent parrots back from his campaign in Africa and India, and no doubt people were keeping birds from the time when man first started to live in fixed settlements. Exactly when aviaries first appeared is not known, but it is generally thought that possibly the Duke de Nivernais may have been the original true aviculturist. He lived near Paris and he had a small wood totally covered in netting in order that he could spend his time among the many birds which he introduced into this enormous aviary. This would mean that modern aviculture dates from the 1700s, earlier references being to birds housed in cages.

It became very fashionable for the nobility of Europe to build ornate aviaries in which to house parrots, birds of prey, and other large avians. When the London Zoo first opened its gates to the public in April 1828, the people were no doubt amazed at the sight of the gaudy macaws on view. At that time the only birds kept by the working class were canaries, which were very popular, and remain so to this day, together with various species indigenous to the country in question.

The budgerigar was undoubtedly the bird that first captured the public's imagination as a "foreign" bird that could be bred in captivity, and probably

Macaws, thanks to their size, coloration, and habits, have always been quick to attract popular attention.

dubious credit in this aspect can be given to Christian Jamrach, a London animal dealer of some fame in his day, who in 1861 purchased no fewer than 3,000 of these birds which arrived on board the "Orient" and "Golden Star" from Australia.

Once the budgerigar had become established, it was not long before more delicate birds attracted the attention of breeders—and so interest grew in those species which were the easiest to maintain. These are, of course, the finches. However, the use of the term "breeders" is rather questionable, as for many years the vast majority of foreign birds imported into Europe and the U.S.A. were never used for breeding but were merely colorful occupants of aviaries.

A number of factors—color, availability, breeding biology, and ease of keeping—contributed to the increase of Budgerigars in captivity.

Even today, far more foreign birds are

Zebra Finches: Chestnut-flanked White above, Pied below.

imported than are bred—with one important exception, which is in respect of the birds of Australia. In 1960 Australia banned the export of all of its wildlife and this prompted people to attempt to build up stocks by breeding. Just how successful they have been can be judged from the fact that the Zebra Finch is now regarded as being fully domesticated and is the least expensive of any birds kept in captivity. A number of other Australian finches are now bred in considerable numbers, as are a select few of other species from Africa, Asia, the U.S.A., and South America. Today, there is a growing awareness that we cannot keep taking birds from the wild, as many are now endangered, and even in cases where they are not, there is the real possibility that countries of origin will eventually ban the export of their birds.

Bird breeding, as opposed to bird keeping, is thus now the priority, and finches are the ideal birds with which a beginner can make a start. Unlike many parrot species, which are noisy and destructive, finches are quiet and can be kept in planted aviaries. Thus they will not only enhance your yard or garden, but will usually be popular with your neighbors, rather than a source of complaint which can be the case with many parrot-like birds.

Many species are available at very modest sums and, once acclimatized, are hardy and can be kept in unheated shelters during the colder months of the more

Fawn Zebra Finch.

temperate and northerly countries of Europe and the U.S.A. Species which are indigenous to either the United Kingdom or the U.S.A. cannot be kept in aviaries or taken from the wild, though in the U.K. strains which are closed ringed and have been bred for generations in captivity are available to aviculturists. Bird breeders in Australia are fortunate in that

Above: Red-cowled Cardinal.
Below: Cinnamon Warbling Finches.

many of their beautiful birds are available to them at only modest prices but, because of the import bans, stocks of non-Australian species are often low or not available; thus prices can be expensive. However, a number of popular species have become well established and are thus reasonable in price.

The term "finch" is strictly applicable only to the birds of the family Fringillidae, but in aviculture it has a much wider application and is used to identify many species which are small seedeaters. In this book, members of the related families Emberizidae (buntings), Estrildidae (waxbills and mannikins) and Ploceidae (weavers and sparrows) will be included.

Ornithologists have long argued over the

exact relationship of many bird species, and certainly the finchlike birds are still the center of much debate. For example, sparrows were originally classed as true finches but are now placed with the weaver birds. The aviculturist is not so much concerned with the scientific status of the birds he or she keeps, but more with how the birds feed or breed under captive conditions. It is nonetheless useful to understand how scientists classify birds, as this can be of immense value when reading through both avicultural and ornithological texts and so, apart from including coverage of the practical aspects of keeping finches, the species chapter includes a basic introduction to the classification of birds.

Above: Bronze-winged Mannikin.
Below: White-headed Nun.

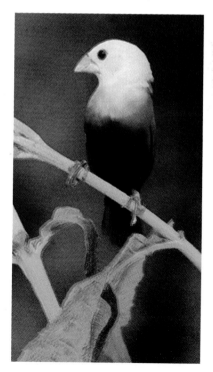

Accommodation

Birds can be housed in aviaries, birdrooms or cages and these will be dealt with in that order. However, before deciding on the type of accommodation to be used, the beginner should consider which species of birds are to be kept. Do you plan to have a single aviary containing a mixed collection or maybe you wish to colony breed with just one species—you may want to breed two or three species? These factors will need to be considered, because based on them, you will decide whether you want one large aviary or two or more smaller ones. It will certainly pay you to visit people who have aviaries, as from these you can note design faults and virtues. There are many commercially made aviaries available and you may decide that they

will suit your needs—or it may be better to build your own. The same is true of cages if you wish to have only one or two pairs of birds in your home as pets. If you are a handy person there is no doubt that self-made aviaries and cages are the cheaper alternative and they can, of course, be fashioned to meet your specific situation.

AVIARIES

The main objective of an aviary is that it will keep the birds in while keeping wild birds and other unwanted visitors out. It should contain an enclosed shelter where the birds can feed and roost and, in most cases, will also be required to store your bird seed and equipment. It is less

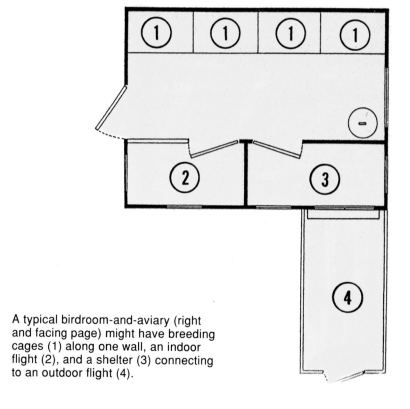

A typical birdroom-and-aviary (right and facing page) might have breeding cages (1) along one wall, an indoor flight (2), and a shelter (3) connecting to an outdoor flight (4).

The outdoor portion of bird accommodations is enclosed with wire mesh, furnished with perches, and might have a door for easy access. Thus the occupants have access to the benefits of fresh air and sunshine on fine days.

The birds can retreat into the shelter section through a flap door; this door also allows the keeper to prevent them from going out if the weather is poor. Some space in the shelter may be devoted to storage for food and equipment.

expensive to build an aviary of simple design than one which is complex, and often visually more pleasing. Size will be of importance in that it will determine the number of birds that it can accommodate in safety—that is, before overcrowding results in serious fighting and injury, as opposed to squabbling of a minor and quite normal level. A common failing of beginners is that they attempt to keep too many birds in too small an aviary and also that they leave insufficient flying room because they try to fill up the aviary with perches and plants.

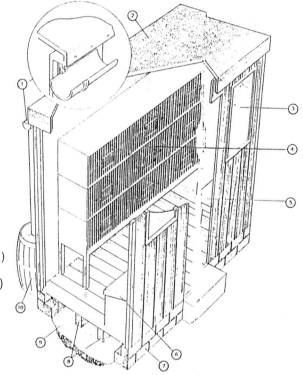

Birdroom details: (1) gutter; (2) sloping roof; (3) window; (4) cages; (5) work table; (6) storage bin; (7) brickwork; (8) beams; (9) concrete; (10) rainwater collector.

Planning

You would not just start building a house without first drawing up plans of its design and location, yet it is surprising just how many aviaries have obviously been erected without any prior thought to their site and structure. The amazing thing is that some of them even stay up for longer than the first strong wind! It is always wiser to delay purchasing birds for that extra period of time, if cash is minimal, in order to invest in solid and attractive aviaries, rather than to cut building costs in order to be underway sooner; your enjoyment will be all the better for having aviaries planned and constructed correctly.

Select a level site away from overhanging trees and which will have the aviary facing south or southeast in order to receive maximum sunshine. Those in the

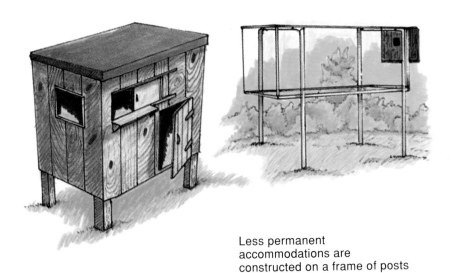

Less permanent accommodations are constructed on a frame of posts set into the ground.

Aviary consisting of three sections, each with an outdoor flight and a shelter.

southern hemisphere will need to reverse this to north or northeast. Overhanging branches from trees reduce sunlight, create more dampness, and wild birds perching above the aviary will foul it with their droppings. Further, any perching owls or hawks will unsettle your birds. Aviaries can be built against existing walls to good effect, but the disadvantage is that mice and cats can more easily sit on these, again disturbing the birds if not actually posing a physical threat to them.

The quietest spot in the garden is best and ideally it should be within view of your favored room. Consideration of the ease with which services, such as light and water, can be supplied should be made as these will be most helpful to you when doing routine jobs. Assuming space permits, allow for possible additional aviaries or a birdroom to be added at a later date if you become a committed aviculturist.

Draw up working plans of the aviary construction, as possible problems might become apparent and it is better to make adjustments on the drawing board than on the actual site. You can also estimate cost of the structure at this stage.

The Base

The actual aviary floor can be of bare earth, but this is difficult to keep clean, can harbor disease for long periods, and can be burrowed through by mice, rats, foxes, and other dangerous animals. A quarter-inch wire mesh could be laid first and then earth and gravel put on top of this, the latter of medium grade to a depth of four inches. The wire will prevent even baby mice entering, while the gravel is neat and easy to rake over to keep clean. Obviously, the ultimate in keeping vermin out, and hygiene of the highest order, is to lay a bed of concrete (preferably one which has been reinforced with fine mesh), and to add a surface layer of gravel for attractiveness. Plants can be grown in tubs and are thus movable should you want a change or should you move to another home. The concrete is best extended beyond the actual aviary site as this can be used a base for a path of slabs or gravel around the perimeter. A very small slope should be made when laying the concrete in order that rain or hose water will run away the shelter end and out a channel at the perimeter. Ensure that the outlet hole from the aviary is well meshed to prevent vermin entering the aviary via it.

Floor plan of an aviary with domed skylights that allow light to enter the shelters.

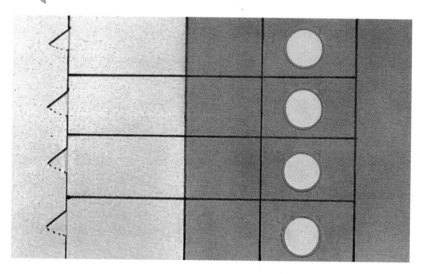

The Aviary

Experience has taught me that it is better to construct the aviary from panels of mesh built onto wooden frames, rather than to simply staple netting onto a pre-erected wooden frame. The reason for this is my wife's periodic desire to move, which has prompted me (and no doubt many others) to think in terms of having as much as possible in a movable state! The panels are simply bolted together and have the added advantage of being easier to replace should any become damaged. One can also increase the flight area without too much trouble simply by bolting on new panels. The bolts are sunk flush with the battens and removed with a box wrench. The panels can either be fixed directly to the concrete base or to a small wall of three or four courses of bricks. To do this, simply sink a bolt, head first, into the concrete, leaving enough exposed thread to go through the aviary mesh frame. The frame is best made from wood of a minimum thickness of two inches, which is strong enough to withstand hard wear and will take a substantial bolt, something which thinner wood will not. The frame is best treated with creosote or one of the preservative paints, prior to the netting being stapled to it. Although it is possible to use one inch netting, this will not prevent mice from entering, nor will it contain the very small finches, so it is recommended that you purchase aviary welded wire of one- quarter inch. This will normally be 23G(gauge), and on rolls 36 inches wide. You should, of course, decide on the width of mesh to be used before assembling the frames, 36 inches and 48 inches being the most convenient to work with. The gauge of wire indicates its thickness and 23 or 19 is suitable, the lower numbers being used for birds such as the parrots.

From a visual viewpoint, the minimum height of the aviary should be six feet, six inches, because if it is lower than this your view will be interrupted by the roofline. It also pays to paint the wire with a dark, lead-free paint as this will make the mesh less noticeable. For those living in more northerly countries where the winter, and even spring, can be very frosty, cold, and wet, transparent panels of Plexiglas are useful extras which can be screwed onto the side panels and roof of the aviary, thus protecting these and the birds during very bad weather.

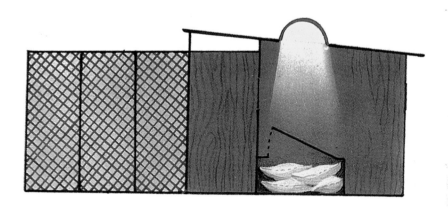

Elevation of an aviary, showing mesh-enclosed flight and shelter with domed skylights.

The Shelter

This structure may simply be large enough to give the birds overnight roosting and feeding space, or it can be a complete birdroom, where you can store seed, have indoor pens, and ample working space for yourself. Again, it can be built from framed panels on which are fitted tongued and grooved slats of wood. The inner side can be lined with plasterboard or simply thin chipboard, and the space between these walls filled with insulating material. It is advised that the shelter be raised above ground level by being placed on cement blocks, thus making it difficult for vermin to hide and so that air can circulate to prevent the wooden floor from rotting. You may, of course, build directly on a concrete base and cover this with tiles or a good quality linoleum that is easy to wash down—which wood is not. The roof of the shelter should slope and be covered with heavy-duty roofing material; it should overhang the shelter walls and contain guttering to take away rainwater.

The addition of electric, water, and even a drain is most useful. Do remember that when brick construction and/or utility services are to be a feature of your aviary, in most countries building permits will be needed, so these should be obtained before you commence building. The aviary wall of the shelter should contain one or more entrance holes for the birds to come through, and it is useful if these have a sliding door which can be locked at night. It will be very convenient if this door can be closed from outside the aviary.

The shelter should be light and airy, so include as many windows as possible—birds do not like to fly into darkened areas. The windows should be covered with a frame of wood and mesh so those which may escape the pen area of the shelter cannot dash themselves against the glass. In warm weather the windows can also be opened. Air vents high up and lower down will assist in fresh air circulation—but make sure they have small grills so mice cannot get in, and they should have a "closed" facility on them. It is useful to have an all-wire inner door to the shelter so that when the outer door is opened, you have a full view of the inside before actually going in—if any birds are loose you can enter without risking their escape. Alternatively, a large glass panel in the

Pair of Zebra Finches, *Poephila guttata*.

door is the next best thing. A safety porch is also advised for the aviary itself. This is simply a small wire-enclosed porch outside of the aviary that enables you to enter this first, before opening the aviary door, thus minimizing the risk of birds escaping as you enter.

Security

If you have built on a concrete base, then this will be as good a safeguard as any against animals burrowing into the aviary. If you have not built on concrete, then a length of fine mesh should be sunk into the ground and turned at right angles away from the flight. This should be done around the entire perimeter, a minimum of one foot down, and one foot outwards. This will not prevent all burrowing but will be a help. Of course, mice, rats, and such can both climb and jump, thus only small size weld wire will be really effective. If traps are set, ensure these are not placed where a bird can become the victim! By keeping everything very neat and tidy, you will at least reduce the risk of vermin becoming established and living to a high standard at your expense.

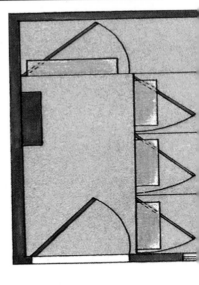

In certain areas, owls and birds of prey can be a menace; rooks and crows can also unsettle birds. In Australia I am told that butcher birds are the worst of all and will grasp birds through the mesh—another good reason for fine mesh, or double netting (on either side of the frames.) The most likely thing to happen is that these birds will alight on the aviary roof and this can be discouraged by covering the aviary with plastic netting suspended about six inches above it. This will "give" under the weight of large birds and as they do not like feeling unsupported, will usually avoid it. Wattling can be placed over a third of the aviary roof and this gives shade and at least hides intruders from the finches' view— up to a point. Fine mesh

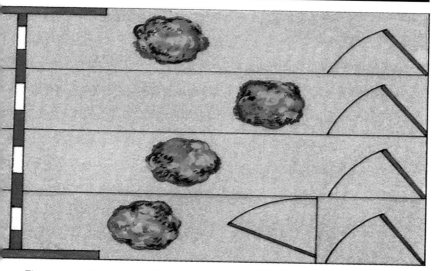

Floor plan of an aviary: this design provides flights and shelters of various sizes to better accommodate different species.

that "gives" will also dissuade cats from walking along the roof.

Human intruders are becoming the worst of all, so all doors should be fitted with good padlocks. It will be worthwhile having an alarm system fitted that rings on your house wall—and a spotlight to light up the aviaries in the event of intruders. A good guard dog is also a very powerful deterrent.

Aviary Fittings

The aviary will require a number of perches of varying thickness and these are best made from branches of fruit trees. Do not include so many that flying space is restricted—fewer will be needed if the aviary is planted. A bath will be appreciated by the birds and this is best made from concrete or similar material rather than those of plastic which are very slippery for birds. Depth should be minimal, say sloping to one inch, and one or two stones in this will

Jar-type dispensers may
be used for food or water
as well.

prefer their birds to have a few plants, weeds or grass growing in the aviary then one or more (depending on aviary size) troughs can be made with bricks or even wood. These can be filled with earth somewhat in the manner of a window box and can look attractive as well as giving the birds areas to peck about in.

Food and water can be supplied in small earthenware pots or in the automatic hopper-type feeders. In an aviary situation it is probably better to feed seed in separate pots, as in this way the birds can select the seed they prefer. Hoppers can easily become clogged, thus appearing to be full, but may not be dispensing the seed, which means you are forever checking that they are working alright. Birds will tend to throw out the seeds they do

give extra landing spots. One placed at ground level and one at a higher level will give the birds a choice.

A shelf to stand nestboxes on can be fitted in the aviary if you plan to colony breed and if the weather in your country is reliable. Other keepers will not like if these are mixed in a hopper, so this is another disadvantage of these feeders. Those designed for water are better and can be clipped at various locations around the aviary and in the shelter. Another type of dispenser for seed is an inverted jam jar which stands on a wooden or plastic base—these can be made or purchased in your local petstore. They are more reliable than the narrow opening hoppers because the aperture is larger. Seed pots must be blown daily to remove the husks from the pot which otherwise appears to be full.

A bird net will be needed for those with aviaries and large pens. A selection of these can be seen at specialist stores. A net is the safest way to catch a bird as the risk of damage is minimal.

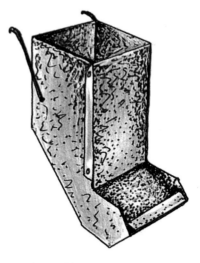

A seed hopper helps to ensure that a supply of food is available at all times.

Night Light

A considerable number of birds die each year in aviaries as a result of night-fright. If disturbed by a sudden noise, such as dogs or a car door slamming, or if startled by car headlights, birds will panic and dash themselves against windows or the aviary wire. This is simply overcome by fitting a low wattage bulb or a blue light in order that the birds can see where they are flying. Further, once on the shelter floor they can then return to their perch without difficulty. The operating costs are negligible.

Plants

There are many plants and shrubs that will enhance an aviary and a list of suggestions is given. Many readers may well be keen gardeners so will know far better than I the varying qualities of these. Beyond their visual appeal in blending the aviary in with the rest of the garden, plants will make good nesting sites and will attract many insects on which the birds can feed. Nor is it essential that all the plants are planted, as a number of species of conifer will survive for quite some time if branches of them are simply attached to the aviary wire or under the covered part of it.

Tree branches add a touch of naturalness to a bird flight.

Planting Suggestions

For screens and possible nesting sites, any of the conifers will be suitable: *Cupressus macrocarpa* is fast-growing though not especially hardy; *C.lawsoniana* and *C.erecta* are nice alternatives. *Lonicera*

Seed dispenser suitable for a collection of finches.

honeysuckle, clematis, jasmine or knotweed. These should be cut back very severely each year and the condition of the aviary wire checked. They will provide nest sites and attract varied insect life, while their flowers will add decoration. In warmer climates, banana plants, magnolia, and non-thorny palms may be tried. In Australia, tea trees of the genus *Leptospermum;* bottlebrushes, *Callistemon;* paperbark, *Melaleuca;* and looking-glass bushes, *Coprosma,* are all popular with aviculturists.

Privet, *Ligustrum:* broom, *Sarothamnus;* gorse, *Ulex;* and hawthorn, are standard bushes used in aviaries. The potential list is almost endless and a chat with your local nurseryman would be worthwhile because he

nitida will make a dense hedge for nesting sites—clip it well back in the spring and autumn. Japanese cedar, *Cryptomeria japonica, is* another plant that will grow densely but which can be trimmed to suit your needs. *Berberis aquifolium is* an evergreen that is very hardy and accepts most soils.

Climbing plants that can be used to effect are

The male Cutthroat Finch, *Amadina fasciata.*

can advise you on the soil of your area which will obviously dictate the most suitable plants to grow.

BIRDROOMS

Should your aviary have only a small shelter, then an additional birdroom will very convenient. This can be newly built or converted outdoor shed—or maybe you have a spare room in the home that could be remodeled. The essentials are that it should be well-ventilated, but not drafty, and contain as many windows as possible so it allows in plenty of light. Floors should be well-covered so they can be kept clean, and walls should be as smooth as possible for the same reason. Should natural sunlight be limited through lack of windows then the use of broad spectrum fluorescent tubes will be better than normal strip lights, as the former emit a light that is more like sunlight. Consult your local lighting specialist on these tubes.

The birdroom can contain one or more large flight pens and numerous stock or breeding cages. A useful extra in a birdroom is an ionizer, which will keep the air fresher and reduce the risk of disease. These can be purchased from specialty dealers who advertise in the various cage birds magazines. The running costs are very low so they are a good investment. It will be found that some form of heating is beneficial—as much for your comfort as for any needs of the birds, but do not have the birdroom too hot. If the heater is wired through a thermostat, this will be ideal, as the one thing you do not want is fluctuations in temperature. A thermometer should also be hung up in the room so you can check that the temperature is being maintained to the correct level in the colder months.

African Silverbill, *Lonchura cantans.*

CAGES

There is no shortage of cage designs available today, but those used by breeders will be box style, and have changed little over the years. Although many ornate cages are made for house birds, I have yet to see one that I would feel happy about housing finches in. Most are woefully small, and seem to be designed more for their appearance rather than practical use. Especially bad are the tall circular type which offer no benefits at all to pet birds. I have always felt that unless pet birds can be given roomy accommodation then they should not be kept.

Apart from any other consideration they are just not seen at their best in cramped cages. If you would like to keep one or two pairs of finches in your home, then it is much better to build your own cage, either a large box type or maybe utilize an alcove which needs only an attractive frame duly

Bird nets are available in various sizes and handle lengths.

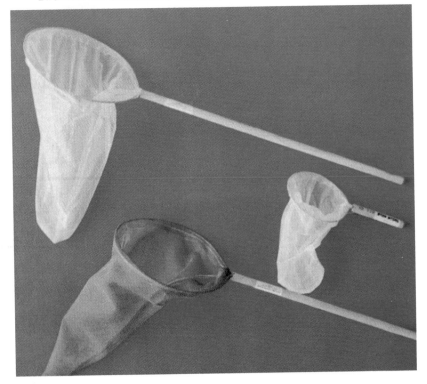

Singly kept finches may become tame enough to be allowed out of their cages.

meshed to be an integral part of your room. Box cages can be made using one of the coated chipboards and these are very easy to wipe clean. Cage fronts can be purchased in various sizes and the cage made to fit these. Finches are better placed in this type of cage because it gives them greater security than the all-wire type. The minimum dimensions I would recommend are 24 x 15 inches for a pair of finches. The actual flying space will be somewhat greater than this, as the size quoted is a standard finch front and allowance must be made for a sliding tray to remove droppings, while sides and top can be such that the wire

Choose the cage—whether it is for transport, exhibition, or breeding—that best suits your needs.

front is placed into a frame which is then inserted into the cage. This will look more attractive than if the front is placed directly into the box cage. Two perches should be fitted as well as food and water pots or hopper type feeders. The cage floor can be lined with newspaper to facilitate ease of cleaning.

Specialist suppliers may well have a number of cages of this style on offer, either in unpainted state or finished in black with white interiors.

Breeder Cages These can be single, double or triple breeders—the latter two usually coming complete with removable sliding partitions so they can be used as one long stock cage or split into two or three separate units. If you plan to have a number of birds, then it is wise to have at least two or three triple cages which can be placed in tiers; these will be needed to accommodate youngsters as well as breeding pairs.

Show Cages Even if you do not plan to exhibit your birds it is wise to have one or two finch show cages which are useful for transporting birds.

Those made for Zebra Finches are ideal and comprise a small box cage with a handle hold in the top and a small circular door in the side.

Designed for canaries, the double-breeder cage is suitable housing for many finch species as well.

Stock Selection

There are numerous factors which will determine the choice of species to be kept, and these will range from the price of the birds, their availability, through to their breeding potential. Compatibility will be a major consideration, but before all else will be the health of the birds so this is where we shall commence.

Bird owners today are fortunate in that until strict quarantine regulations were adopted, the purchase of freshly imported birds, especially small finches, was a risky business. These birds have amazing powers of recovery in a very short time—but they can as easily die in a matter of hours, especially from stress and starvation following a long journey—this was often the case. Happily, importers now have to retain stocks for a number of weeks to ensure there is no risk that disease can be introduced to a country. This means that the birds you can purchase are at least feeding and are the tougher of those originally shipped because they have survived their journey and the quarantine period.

However, this does not mean they are fully fit, acclimatized or feeding correctly. These comments do not apply to Australian finches purchased outside of that country simply because all such birds will have been bred in captivity, Australia having banned bird export in 1960. Although some of their species may have been exported from Japan or

Chestnut-breasted Mannikin, *Lonchura castaneothorax*.

A HEALTHY BIRD

When looking at birds, there are a number of telltale signs to help decide if they are healthy. Obviously, if a bird is chirpy and hopping from perch to perch, that is a good sign for openers. Beware, however, of the bird that you have startled into action and who might not be well, but moves out of fear. The eyes should be round and clear of any discharge or swelling. Partially closed eyes indicate a problem. The beak should be well formed with no signs of damage. The vent should be clean and not stained or clogged with feces. The legs and toes should show no signs of swelling and there should be three forward and one backward facing toes. Any toes that are missing or deformed may not affect the day to day well-being of the

elsewhere, nonetheless they were captive bred and are thus hardy. The same comment applies in reverse to Australians, that is, non-indigenous species of foreign birds must have been bred in Australia as imports are also banned.

bird, but they could affect its ability to perch correctly when breeding, so we will avoid these.

The feathers should be neat, clean, and fit tightly against the body. It is possible that recently imported birds might still look a bit

Java Sparrow, *Padda oryzivora.*

bedraggled and these will molt out just fine; even so, caution should be exercised for they might have a feather problem. Any bird that sits on its perch all fluffed up and takes no notice of you when you approach has a problem, so it is not for you. Take a good look at the droppings in the cage to see if there are signs of unduly copious or green feces as this could indicate intestinal problems with the birds. It is obviously better to take someone along with you who has kept birds for some time, but if not, then be extra choosy over the birds before you part with hard-earned dollars.

WHERE TO BUY

Pet shops or breeders are the best sources of supply. The establishment should be very clean, the cages likewise, and the attendants should be neat, helpful and know their business. A breeder should have tidy aviaries which are not overcrowded and the stock cages should be smart and clean.

If you are thinking in terms of finches, such as Gouldian or parrot finches, then purchasing from a specialist breeder of these birds is the best way. You are strongly advised to visit one or more bird shows before buying stock, as in this way you may well locate a local breeder of the species you are interested in. In any case, at such venues you can see what really fit and fully plumed birds should look like.

In most countries, there are avicultural magazines in which will be found interesting articles so subscription to one is recommended. Bird clubs are an excellent way to gain knowledge as well as

Parrot-billed Seedeater, *Sporophila peruviana.*

friends, so joining one will be most rewarding.

It is possible to have birds sent to you via carriers, but for myself I always prefer to collect my own. This way I see what I am buying and if what I want is not available locally, then I will make a buying trip

Purple Grenadier,
Uraeginthus ianthinogaster.

to one of the larger specialists in birds.

Prices

These will reflect availability, species in question, and the status of the birds.

Availability Certain species are imported in vast numbers each year and so are inexpensive. These will tend to be the less colorful birds, though this is a relevant term as many are very pleasing. Possibly the least expensive of all birds is the Zebra Finch, which is so well established as a prolific breeder that currently pairs can be purchased cheaper than imported common wild species. Birds are imported at different times of the year, so prices "out of season" will be higher than when large numbers are available. Another factor that will affect availability is when a species is suddenly banned from being exported; at such times prices will soar.

Certain of the smaller exporting countries can be unreliable as to supplies, perhaps due to internal politics or to the lack of established long-term traders in birds. As a result, there can be a glut of certain species for a while and then nothing, so this affects the price in the store.

Birds which are of a color mutational form will always be more expensive than the normal or wild type simply because there are fewer of them. The rarer the mutation, the more costly it is.

Above: Golden-breasted Bunting. **Below:** Crested Chocolate Bengalese Finches.

Species As a rule of thumb, the larger the species the more expensive it will be, and if the bird is rarely imported, or there are few of them, then these too will be more costly. For example, the buntings of the Americas will be more expensive than popular small finches of Africa or Asia. Redbrowed Waxbills, though small, are fewer in number than Gouldians, and will be up to three or four times their price.

Status If the age and sex of a bird is known, then this will affect its price. Obviously, in captive-bred species the ages are known but not always the sex as many finches are not dimorphic, which means the male and female are not similar in appearance. It is possible to surgically sex larger birds and this is a common practice in parrots, but is costly and very difficult in smaller birds. Feces can be microscopically analyzed but this is also expensive, so when a true pair is known they will be more expensive than normal "pairs", which does not always imply one of each sex.

The first finch to become popular as a cage bird was the wild Canary, *Serinus canaria.*

Fawn-and-White Bengalese Finches.

When a bird is captive-bred, it will always be higher priced than its wild counterpart simply because it will be fully acclimatized, feeding well, and be in excellent health. Such birds, though more costly, are much the better investment.

PET BIRDS

If it is your desire to simply purchase a pair of birds, or maybe two pairs, then it is best to acquire popular species that are captive-bred, are true pairs, and are compatible. This is much better than just having all cocks, because their plumage is more colorful—and bear in mind that certain species, such as Orange Bishops, only sport their glorious colors (cocks) during the period of breeding; at other times they are rather

Gouldian Finch, *Chloebia gouldiae*, a male of the red-headed morph.

can be established.

Likewise, the days of bachelor-only mixed collections I think are numbered, and those with aviaries are recommended at least to attempt to breed their birds. This may mean fewer species can be kept but you are well compensated by the thrill of having bred your birds rather than continually taking them from the wild. Compatibility is discussed in the chapter on breeding. A selection of the more readily available species, plus a few that are less frequently seen, are described in the species chapter, which also gives an indication, in a general sense, of prices.

drab, like the hen. In this age of animal conservation it is perhaps egotistical for us to keep pairs of high-priced rare birds in cages without attempting to breed from them, so such birds are best left to aviculturists in order that homebred strains

TRANSPORTING BIRDS

Most establishments will provide you with small cardboard containers specially made for carrying birds, but if you have already purchased a show cage or similar suitable container then take this with you. I have one in the car trunk at all times. I also have a small homemade carrier that can be divided into four sections with slide-in aluminum partitions; this is very handy if I know I will be purchasing a few pairs of birds.

If the journey is a long one then ensure you have a hopper style water bottle fitted as the birds will likely get thirsty. Seed can be scattered on the cage floor. Always try to collect birds as early in the day as possible so you are home early, and the birds can settle into their "quarantine" cage or pen and feed before nighttime. Should you arrive home in the evening then keep your birdroom light on later than normal.

The Diamond Firetail, *Emblema guttata*, is a stolid bird, very intolerant of others when inclined to breed.

ACCLIMATIZATION

Never put freshly acquired birds directly into an established aviary as this can introduce disease. They must first be isolated for a minimum of two weeks so that any problems have time to show themselves. Ideally, additional birds should be housed away

Gouldian Finch, *Chloebia gouldiae*, black-headed male.

temperatures are quite high, and while a degree of acclimatization takes place at this time, it is by no means sufficient for your purposes. Further acclimatization takes place once birds are purchased by pet stores, but again, unless you live in a very warm country, you will still need to slowly reduce the room temperature of your isolated birds until it corresponds with that of your aviaries. While in isolation you can monitor which seeds the birds are eating and also make adjustments to their diets if this was spartan (which is usually the case in imported birds).

from all other stock, but often this is not possible, so keep special cages for this purpose and ensure they are well cleaned after each use and are not re-used for at least ten days.

Freshly imported birds are normally housed in quarantine stations where the room

Once you are satisfied that all is well with your new arrivals, they can be released into the aviary, but will still need observing to ensure that they know where the feeding stations are. Also, if they are additions to an existing aviary community, take special notice of how they are accepted by the other birds. Just because one of the species lived happily alongside other species does not mean another of the same species will. Finches are no different from other animals and every one is an individual.

Above: Lavender Finch.
Below: Red-billed Firefinch pair.

Feeding

The feeding of most species of birds has improved considerably over the years and this has stimulated far greater success in breeding. The days of simply giving one's birds a seed mixture, a water pot, and occasional grit are hopefully over. Such a diet may well keep your birds alive but that does not make it a healthy diet. On this question I am reminded of a wonderful phrase attributed to the 12th Duke of Bedford, an aviculturist of world renown, sadly no longer with us—it is quoted in Jeffrey Trollope's excellent book on seedeating birds (1983). The Duke, in reply to a lady boasting about the longevity of her far-from-healthy parrot, said, "Madam, your parrot has not lived a long time; it's merely taking a long time to die!"

In the wild state, finches live in a range of habitats from grassland to tropical jungle, scrubland to marsh, so have variations in the type of food available to them. Further, their dietary needs differ depending on whether it is the breeding season or not. Likewise, some plants are only available at certain times of the year, so the birds have alternate sources of food at other times. The objective of the aviculturist is to try to provide a diet that as closely resembles the wild one as possible. Clearly, this cannot be duplicated exactly so it is a case of ensuring that the intake of vital consume the same percentage of seed in ratio to other foods, so it is essential that we do not fall into the trap of treating them all the same. For this reason it is worthwhile to keep a notebook in which observations of what each bird prefers is detailed, and from this you will build your own record, which may well prove valuable at a later date. Such a book should also contain notes on how species interact, etc. Our knowledge of captive husbandry is far from complete and progresses only because breeders are prepared to experiment and then record the results for better or worse.

Sundry bird-keeping supplies typically found in a pet shop: breeding cages, wicker nests, food and water cups, and various kinds of seeds.

components of the diet are met within the alternatives available. Remember that all finch species will not

ESSENTIALS OF A DIET

Food can be placed into various groups based on its function within the body.

Normal flying and muscular activity is possible because the energy for this is provided by *carbohydrates* in the diet. Certain seeds, such as canary or millet, are rich in carbohydrates. Bodily growth is accomplished as a result of tissue being built from *proteins*. These are also needed for tissue repair and, of course, by growing chicks. Rape and linseed are rich seed sources of protein, while other sources are milk, cheese and live foods. *Fats* obviously provide insulation, but they furfill other needs, including furnishing a secondary source of energy. In fact, they are more efficient energy producers than

For many finch species, seed mixtures composed mainly of millets are typical. Here, Zebra Finches pick and choose from a tray placed on the cage floor.

carbohydrates; they serve also in helping normal bodily functioning and the absorption of vitamins. Fat-rich foods are rape and sunflower seeds, milk, cheese, and the like.

Although needed in small quantities only, *vitamins* are vital to good health, and a lack of them can result in illness or even death.

Your local pet shop carries a wide variety of vitamin supplements. *Minerals*, such as calcium, phosphorous, copper, and others are often termed "trace elements," and are again vital to healthy condition. *Water* must always be available to your birds—ideally at a minimum of two feeding points—and lack of it will certainly create stress and ill-health. On occasions, the

The White-throated Seedeater, *Sporophila albogularis,* typifies a number of somberly colored New World finches.

availability of water can mean the difference between a bird living or dying, especially when it is unwell and refuses food. It is an ideal way of giving a bird medicines as those in liquid or powder form can be added to the

Commercial tonics and medicines are often sufficient to put minor complaints right.

water in droppings and bodily evaporation to keep cool than is taken in or produced from its food. The daily deficit must be replaced, otherwise the bird's body is forced to draw its needs from the breakdown of bodily tissues; further, the body cannot then function correctly, i.e. defecation becomes difficult, and in turn this creates problems. Overall, no less than 70% of your bird's body is comprised of water, so its importance becomes self-evident. Having discussed food in a general sense, let us now look at the various foods that will make up your birds' menu.

drinking water. Birds gain certain quantities of water from seeds and other foods, and water is also a byproduct of metabolic processes; even so, studies have shown that on any one day a bird will lose more

SEED

Firstly, it is important that only the best quality seeds are fed to your birds, so any that are offered at unusually low prices should be viewed with scepticism. Seed should smell fresh and not be dusty, nor should there be any signs of mold or contamination. It must never be stored in damp conditions, and it is wise to purchase small quantities on a regular basis than to buy in bulk just to save money. Obviously you will take a middle road on this that enables you to have sufficient seed to last a few weeks, rather than months, which increases the risk of the seed going 'off'.

Seed is best stored in metal bins rather than plastic, simply because it will not sweat as readily. Large glass jars are ideal, but getting good-sized ones is difficult. Polyethylene bags are not recommended.

Galvanized cans can be used to store sizeable quantities of seeds and such.

Seed mixtures for finches can be purchased, or you can make up your own blend, which is usually the best policy if a number of birds are kept. Australian finches and certain African species favor canary seed and the various millets (panicum, white, yellow). Canaries and European or North American finches will accept a wider range of seeds, including sunflower, rape, and maw. Sunflower is too large for many species to husk, but if soaked in hot water for a few minutes, it will soften enough for some birds to cope with it. The mix you feed will reflect the overall make-up, by species, of your collection, and it is for this reason that seed is best fed in separate

Many shops have seeds and other supplies available in bulk, so the bird keeper need buy only as much as can be used in a short time.

dishes (or hoppers, if you prefer this type of feeder).

One of the problems birdkeepers are faced with is encouraging their birds to accept seeds they are unaccustomed to, but it is worthwhile trying to persevere in this pursuit. It sometimes happens that seed rejected once will be accepted later, so record the times when seed is rejected. Often, if one bird will take a sample, others will follow. Another method is to withhold normal seeds during the early morning and supply only those which you would like your birds to have. Of course, the birds must not be deprived of their regular seed for too long—just until they may have sampled the introduced seeds.

The seeds of most grasses will be readily

A pair of Jacarini Finches, *Volatinia jacarina.*

taken and these are rich in proteins but be careful where these are gathered, as any that have been treated with chemicals can be very dangerous to your birds.

Breeding birds, as well as those that are unwell, will benefit from germinating seeds, as the protein level in these rises

considerably. To effect the process, place a number of seeds in a small container of tepid water and place this in a warm, darkened spot. After 24 hours, the seeds should be rinsed in fresh water and returned to the same place. After a further 24 hours, the seeds will be ready and should be thoroughly rinsed again (a sieve is best for this). Then allow the seeds to dry for a few hours. In this state, the birds will usually be very keen to consume them. If they are germinated to the point where they start to sprout, this is an excellent way of testing the seeds. Simply count those that have not germinated and if the percentage is high,

Seeds that are fed dry are also suitable for sprouting; placed in soil, they may be allowed to become grasses, which will both be eaten and even used for nesting material.

then maybe you need a new supplier because the seeds are of poor quality.

Any seeds can be fed after germination, but panicum millet and canary seeds are the usual ones. Millet spray can also be given soaked and will be regarded as a special treat.

During the non-breeding season, birds will require few protein seeds as it is essentially energy they need. Prior to the breeding season, and throughout it, they need plenty of body-building proteins, so this is the time when the seeds will be required.

Other types of seed will be seen on merchants' lists.

These are always worthwhile finding out about and trying, provided they are small enough for your finches to cope with.

Pintailed Parrot Finch, *Erythrura prasina*, a male.

GREENFOODS

Greenfoods are essential to birds, as they provide vitamins not always found in seeds. Breeding results can nosedive if greens are not provided during the

While not very colorful, the Owl Finch, *Poephila bichenovii*, is nevertheless thought very attractive by many fanciers.

tops, celery, spinach, and watercress. There really is no limit to the potential range, and of course wild plants such as shepherds purse, milk (sow) thistle, clover, and chickweed are excellent plants that can be fed. Again, care should be taken when gathering wild plants because of the risk of chemical contamination. Many bird breeders grow their own wild plants. Berries and fruits of all kinds eaten by wild birds will be safe and good for your birds. These include blackberry, rose hip, hawthorn, elderberry, and raspberry. All cultivated vegetables should be thoroughly washed before they are fed to the birds. Uneaten food should be removed each day.

breeding season, so always feed a variety of both cultivated and wild greenfoods. Choose those with very green leaves rather than the inner, more yellow leaves.

Excellent examples of these foods are dandelions, carrot

One hears some breeders say that too much greenfood causes

diarrhea in birds, but this is not true—though easy to see why it happens. Supplies of many plants are good during spring and summer, but recede during fall and winter. Birds are given a glut during the good months, then little or none in the colder months. After having received little greenfood, the birds tend to gorge on them when they are again plentiful and this causes diarrhea. The secret is to give the birds a steady supply year round and they will not have the need to overeat this type of food. Alternatively, introduce *extra* greenfoods gradually and likewise reduce them the same way before the season ends so that you are in effect duplicating what would happen in the natural state. Pieces of fresh fruit will be

Larger finch species, such as the Masked Hawfinch, *Coccothraustes personatus*, will of course require larger food items, such as nuts.

appreciated by most birds even though they may not consume large quantities. Make up a fruit salad of finely chopped pieces and feed in pots. Apples can be hung on

Properly stored seed mixtures should remain fresh for some time, but periodical freshness checks are always a good idea.

the aviary wire and will give the birds amusement as well as nutrition.

LIVEFOOD

All finches will benefit from the inclusion of livefood in their diet and it is extremely important for breeding pairs. For many years the stock livefood was either mealworms, which are the larval stage of the beetle *Tenebrio molitor*, or maggots, the larval state of various flies such as the bluebottle, or the greenbottle (termed "pinkies"). Mealworms are liked by most finches but their tough chitin skin is sometimes difficult for the smallest finches to cope with and so breeders will dip them in boiling water to soften this. The young larvae are the best to feed.

Mealworms, maggots, and whiteworms can be purchased from anglers' stores or from pet stores but if purchased from anglers' supplies then do not buy those which have been treated with a color dye. It is probably harmless, but why take chances? Other popular livefoods are crickets, locusts, and fruit flies, as well as so-called ant eggs, which are the cocoons of various ants. Each of these can be purchased from pet stores. Cultures of mealworms and maggots are easily prepared. For maggots simply hang up a piece of meat or fish, wrapped in cheesecloth or similar.

Beneath this place a large tin which is half filled with bran. The maggots will fall from the meat as they grow and should be transferred to fresh bran in order that they excrete any harmful toxin they may have. Some of the maggots may be allowed to pupate in a ventilated box which is placed in the aviary; if the holes are large enough for

Himalayan Greenfinch, *Carduelis spinoides.*

the flies to escape then many will be taken by your birds as they exit from the box.

Mealworms are bred by introducing adult flour beetles into a wooden or plastic box which is lined with hessian and covered with bran to one inch; next, lay paper over the bran and beetles and place chopped pieces of vegetables on this. Lettuce leaves will keep the box humid and these can be placed in as well, then a lid is placed on the box. It will take a few weeks for the larvae to develop and during this time the vegetables and

Millet sprays are relished by finches, perhaps because such foraging seems more natural.

lettuce will need replacing. A warm temperature is needed, about that of a room, and the larvae can be taken as required—some being allowed to pupate in order to start a new culture.

In a mixed collection it will be found that some species will greedily devour mealworms to the extent that other species get none. The answer is not to put more in, as too many are not good for the birds. Observe which are not getting any and see if they can be encouraged to take them from your fingers—if not, then spread them on the aviary floor where even the smallest finch will be able to descend and quickly take one. In actual fact, neither maggots nor mealworms are an especially efficient way of supplying protein,

Bullfinch x canary hybrid.

which is why it pays to supply as wide a variety of livefood as possible.

Another useful way of increasing variety is to cut branches of shrubs and plants which are seen to have various insects on them and hang these in the aviary—where the birds will quickly eat the insects. You can also shake plants over a plastic bag and

INSECTIVOROUS FOODS

There are numerous brands of proprietary insectivorous foods now available to birdkeepers and these are an excellent addition to the diet. Initially, birds may not accept them, but if some livefood is added to the mix this will encourage the birds to sample such foods, after which they will no doubt accept the pure mix.

Ant cocoons are very nutritious and should you not be able to collect these from the wild then dried 'eggs' can be purchased. They can be mixed in with a finch mash after having been soaked in milk. Do remember that milk sours quickly so uneaten mixes must be removed in a relatively short period.

The Star Finch, *Neochmia ruficauda*, is one of the better known of the Australian grass finches.

numerous insects will be collected in this way and these can be placed onto a white plate where they will be spotted by the birds.

MINERALS AND GRIT

Minerals are found in many foods, including seeds and greenfood.

Those which are especially important for birds are calcium, phosphorous, manganese, iodine, cobalt, and zinc. They fulfill a variety of roles and the first two named are vital for the production of good eggshell.

Cuttlefish is a valuable source of calcium and is available from pet stores. It is usually hung from the aviary roof or attached to clips on the aviary wire. It pays also to crush up some cuttlefish and place it in a small pot in the shelter. Most finches will take it in this powdered form. Oyster shell and crushed eggshells are also rich in calcium. One way of ensuring that your birds are not deficient of any minerals is to

Sterilized bone flour	177 g.
Carbonate of lime	1332 g.
Rock or kitchen salt	340 g.
Sulfur	56.7 g.
Ferric oxide	28.35 g.
Manganese hypophosphate	2.8 g.

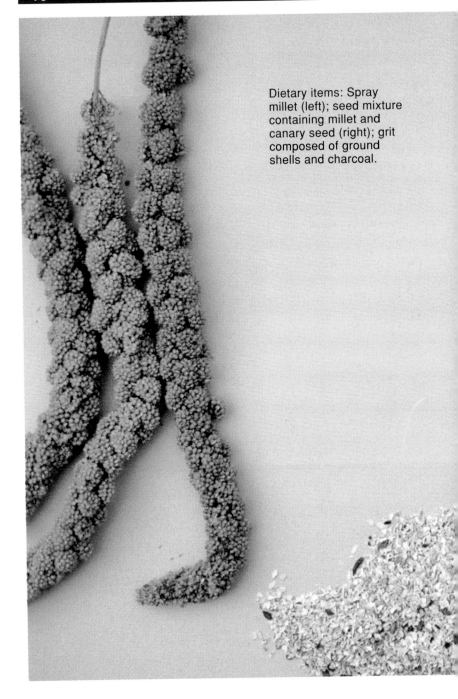

Dietary items: Spray millet (left); seed mixture containing millet and canary seed (right); grit composed of ground shells and charcoal.

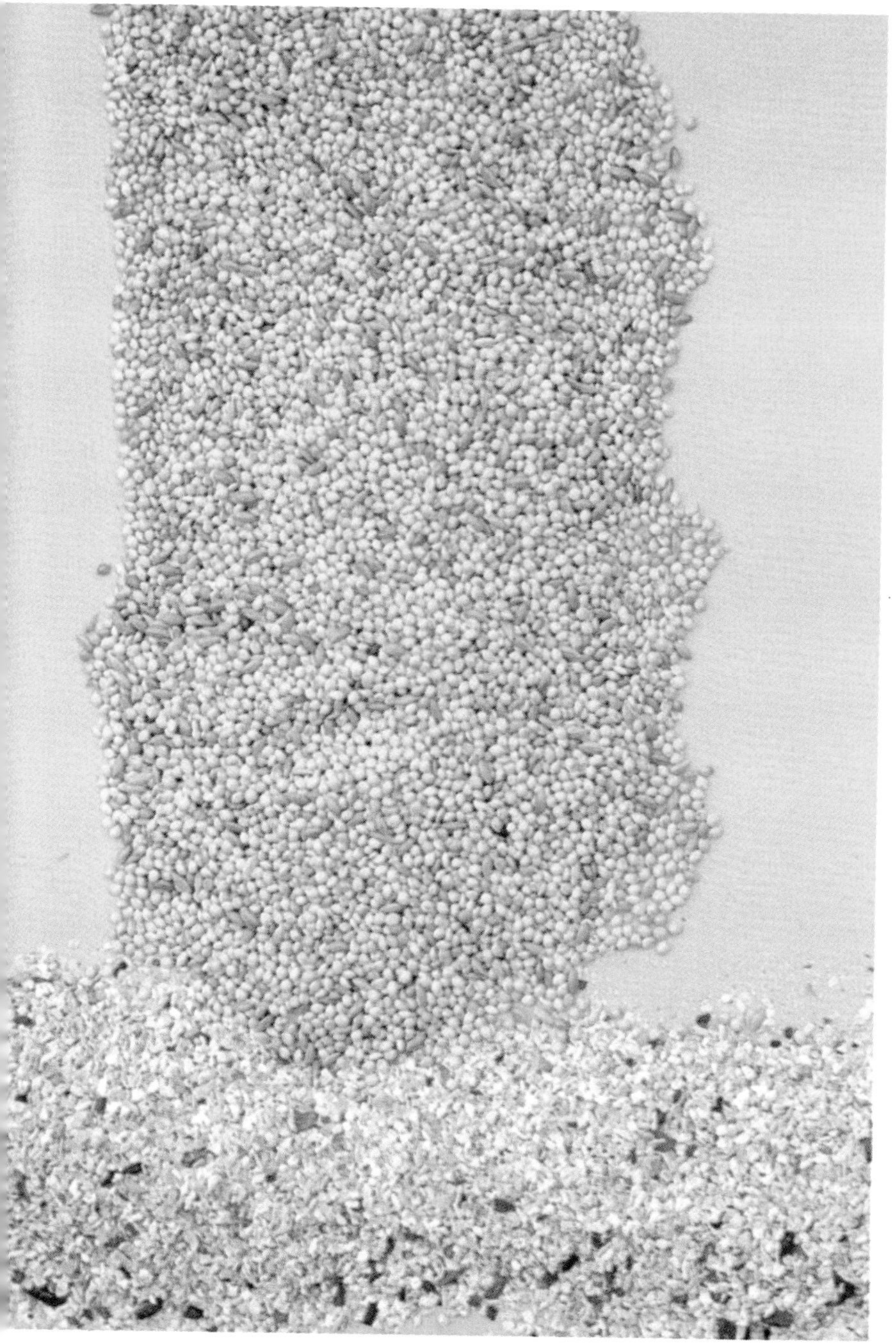

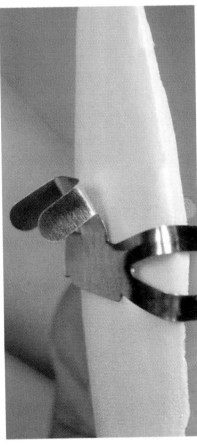

A cuttlefish bone attached to the wire of the enclosure will provide finches with a source of minerals.

main role for finches is to aid in the digestion process. Remember, birds do not possess teeth so the husked seed is broken down by the strong muscles of the gizzard aided by grit, which is thus essential. This can be purchased from your pet store. It can be given in pots or scattered on the aviary floor, or both.

The importance of the inclusion of both greenfood and livefood cannot be overemphasized, especially in the time up to, and throughout, the breeding season. It has been clearly demonstrated time and again that if the diet is deficient in any of the components detailed in this chapter then infertility will increase, dead-in-shell will be more pronounced, and chicks will either be fewer in number or not fed by their parents.

have your pharmacy make up a mixture for you. That quoted below is recommended by the Avicultural Society of Australia.

Grit This provides certain minerals but its

Breeding

One of the charms of breeding finches is that they are far more accommodating than are other groups of birds. Finches are quiet, many are inexpensive, their diet is relatively straightforward, and there are a wealth of species from which to choose, ranging from those which are established and prolific breeders to those which are rarely bred, even though they are imported in vast numbers and are thus not expensive to buy. This is one reason why many of them are ignored by breeders.

An opportunity to bathe can be provided by attaching a bath box to the cage.

Finches can be bred in aviaries or in breeder cages and it is not unknown for pairs of pet birds to rear chicks in the confines of a home.

You may decide you wish to breed exhibition standard birds, or one of the many color mutational forms, or, like this author, prefer to breed birds simply for the challenge of breeding, rather than for the pursuit of goals which might require you to move away from what I would consider are the more important aspects of aviculture. I feel this point is worthy of further comment. One sees in dogs, cats, rabbits, goldfish, and most popular pets, all sorts of monstrosities that are the result of selective inbreeding which has capitalized on mutations as they appear. In birds, one can see it in pigeons, fowl, canaries and, to a much lesser degree, even in budgerigars.

The problem is that the pursuit of the bizarre or unusual takes over to the point that consideration of the animal (or bird) becomes of secondary importance only. Never mind if a dog can hardly breathe, or if a fish has eyes prone to damage from the slightest knock—or if a bird can't rear and feed its own young, or if infertility is on the increase. Never mind if the birds spend their entire lives in breeder cages, because in this way fewer chicks are lost and we can more easily control and increase the number of mutations. At what point do we ask, "What benefit does selective inbreeding of mutants give to the birds being bred and how does it best serve the *long term*

Bengalese Finch nestlings. The feather sheaths start to protrude from the wings several days after hatching.

interests of aviculture as a whole?" I full appreciate that much knowledge is derived from the activities prompted by selective inbreeding, but cannot help thinking that if the abilities and enthusiasm of color breeders and exhibitors were channelled into the establishment of domestic strains of the less-bred species, then this would be to the undoubted benefit of aviculturists generally. Presently, there is a need to establish vigorous strains of even the well-established breeds, such as Gouldian Finches, where one can see strong evidence that the birds are being increasingly bred under very artificial conditions. I see no benefits in this for the future, as it can only result in weaker stock that will present as many problems to those who require aviary birds as if the birds had been imported from the wild.

With respect to those species presently imported in large numbers, but infrequently bred, I believe hard economics is the reason for this. It can take quite some time, and no small expense, to establish domestic strains of wild birds, and if the resulting progeny cannot be sold at a reasonable price, then it becomes difficult to maintain worthwhile programs unless you are especially well-off. However, there are two strong reasons for attempting to establish more domestic species. Firstly, I do not think, in this day and age, we can morally continue to be consumers of wild populations and, secondly, all the signs are with us that sooner or later most species

Well-fed Gouldian Finch nestlings. The hulled, but whole, seed kernels in the chicks' crops are clearly visible through the thin skin.

presently imported will be banned - either by the importing country or the experting nations. When this happens, "common", low-priced species will rapidly become very pricey, and as one cannot tell just when restrictions will be imposed, we should take the opportunity, while we have it, to breed every species that is available to us at this time. You may not be "fashionable," but you will surely be making a very worthwhile contribution to aviculture—and it could just work out to your advantage in the long term.

FITNESS

It is essential that your birds are fully fit before any attempt is made to breed them. In the nonbreeding season this will mean feeding a diet of carbohydrate-rich seeds together with greenfood, vitamin supplement, and minerals. Obese hens will most certainly become eggbound so they must be well exercised. In aviary birds this is less a problem than with cage-bred stock where one should have at least a large pen in which to exercise stock. This is most important should you have no aviary.

A few weeks prior to pairs being introduced, the hen should be given small amounts of soft food (finch mash), or bread and milk, as this will build up her protein and calcium levels in readiness for chick rearing. Likewise, introduce high protein seeds slowly at this time, as well as occasional livefoods.

COMPATIBILITY

It must not be assumed that having a

Zebra Finches still in the nest. Although a clutch of finch eggs all tend to hatch at the same time, differences of only a day or two continue to be evident as the youngsters develop.

true pair of finches will be sufficient to ensure that mating takes place—far from it. Birds have their own very firm views on which of the opposite sex will make a suitable mate, and often this may not coincide with your wishes! For this reason, it is always wiser to introduce pairs weeks, or even months, prior to their being required to breed. If it becomes obvious that the hen is not compatible with the cock, then a new partner should be found for the hen.

The newcomer to aviculture is wiser to commence breeding operations with species that are both proven breeders and also sexually dimorphic, as in this way they will not become frustrated at obtaining true pairs or finding it difficult to encourage them to mate. Experience gained with Zebra Finches, canaries, or Bengalese will prepare the way for more ambitious projects. This does not mean you cannot include another species in your aviary, but most beginners want success and need the experience of positive results, which are virtually assured with birds such as those named. It must also be remembered that in the case of imported birds one is never quite sure how old the birds are, so you could just be devoting a great deal of time to birds that might be too old.

NESTING SITE

A number of finches will utilize one of the varieties of commercially made nestboxes, whereas others prefer to build their own nests. In the case of the former, nestboxes should be placed into position shortly before you wish the birds to mate. This

A Fawn Zebra Finch chick, just at fledging age. Fledging becomes possible when the feathers of the wings and tail have grown to a length able to support flight.

Finch nestlings are completely helpless, relying on their parents for their every need.

usually induces the birds to breed and the cocks will be seen whistling, displaying, and generally courting the hens. The nestboxes should be sited in quiet, sheltered spots in the aviary where they are protected from wind and rain. Select sites reasonably high up and always place at least two nestboxes per pair of birds in order that there is no squabbling over a particular box or site. It is better that one side of the aviary is totally clear of nests and such an area will be used as a social meeting place for all pairs this equating the normal wild situation. Nestboxes can be hung in the shelter as well as in the flights and some pairs will prefer these; indeed, birds will choose the most unusual places to nest at times. It is not unusual to see nests in ceiling joints and even in large feeder pots!

Nesting material in the form of dried grasses, old wild birds' nests, feathers, and similar should be placed at various points and these will be gathered by the birds. Those who build their own nests should be supplied with a good screen of conifer, gorse, privet, or similar location. Even cut branches of these can be fixed to the aviary wire to form a suitable site—they will wither, but do not worry as the birds will attend to their brood provided you do not unduly disturb them. Breeders differ in their attitude on the question of nest inspection, some keeping a very watchful eye on developments, whereas others prefer to leave the birds totally to their own devices. Much will depend on the routine you have already

A clutch of Gouldian Finch eggs—white eggs are characteristic of estrildid finches.

established and how
familiar the birds are
with your presence in
the aviary.

Finches build open
nests, whereas weavers
have elaborate domes
to they will build
totally or they will
build onto nestpans
and for these reasons it
is always wise to
include a variety of
nestbox styles.

In a mixed or
communal aviary,
always watch out for
single birds or pairs
which are very
aggressive towards
others. These should
be removed, as they
can create havoc to
otherwise peaceful
communities. I am not
talking about petty
squabbling, but
habitual intrusions on
the nests of other birds.

TYPES OF BREEDING

All finches do not
breed in the same
manner, by which is
meant that some are

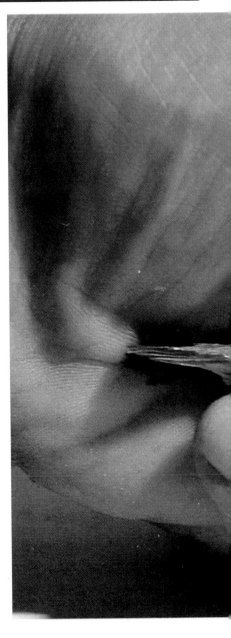

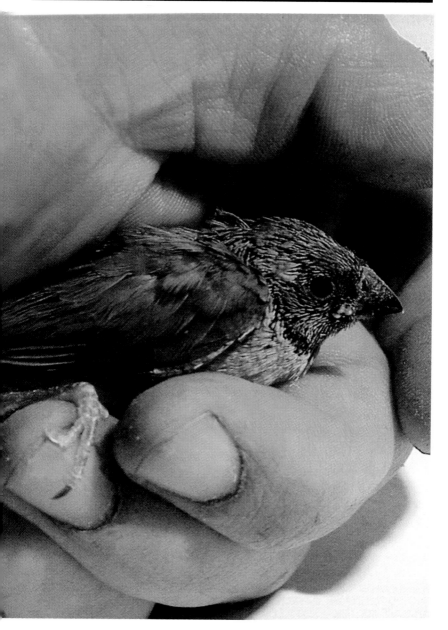

Gouldian Finch nestling, almost fully feathered. The colorful gape tubercules are still visible, but adult feather coloration is still some months away.

very communal, others breed in pairs, while yet others are termed polygamous, in which a male will mate with two or more hens during the breeding season. Examples of these three types are: mannikins are communal breeders; finches breed as pairs, but many will tolerate conspecifics if space permits; and many weavers are polygamous. In the species chapter, reference is made to the social inclinations of the birds covered. As a general rule, if you wish to include a number of finches in an aviary then choose species that are unrelated and show widely differing plumage colors, and also species that differ in their nesting requirements, thus removing potential sources of squabbling.

A pair of Gouldian Finches, the male being the Blue-breasted variety. A nest box affixed to the outside of the cage and accessible through a hole in the wire is desirable because it does not diminish the cage space available for exercise.

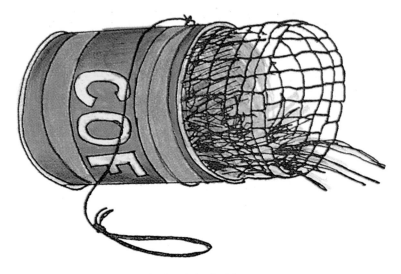

Coffee-can nest site furnished with some grasses.

The more delicate species might require heated shelters in the northern states. Some may well need heated birdrooms to induce breeding, especially species that are recently imported or not regarded as especially prolific. Once you have successfully bred such birds, then in the following season attempt to breed some of your stock in the aviary, as it is in this way that hardy strains are developed that will one day form the nucleus for that species in aviaries, as opposed to always remaining birdroom breeders. Obviously, you should keep notes on all pairs and happenings as this will be more easily checked, and essential material in you can control which compiling your history of birds mate with which. the birds vou are breeding.

CAGE BREEDING

The advantage of cage breeding is that less hardy birds can be bred, a closer watch can be kept on matters, nestboxes are more easily checked, and you can control which birds mate with which. This is, of course, most important if one is producing any of the color mutatuions seen in Zebra Finches, Gouldians, Bengalese, and numerous others.

The double or triple breeder cages should be used and two perches are placed, one at each end, and at differing heights. Nestboxes are best placed outside the cage, the fronts being cut to accommodate them, but they are fine inside as well—though nest inspection is much more difficult in such cases. Nesting material should be placed on the cage floor—but not under perches where it can be soiled; some can be pushed into the nestbox. The cock is always placed into the cage first and the hen the following day. Check that they are compatible. They will then commence

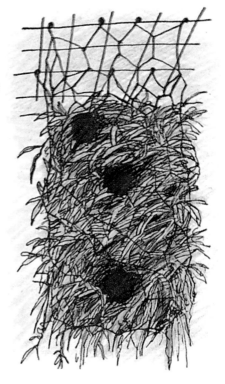

Finches will make nest holes in a bunch of grass hung near the aviary roof.

The Black-tailed Lavender Waxbill, *Estrilda perreini*, has seldom been imported and therefore rarely bred in captivity.

courting displays and the pair will sit close to each other when not active. If you place a wire divider between a pair in the first instance then you will be able to observe if they are clearly wishing to be together and the divider can be removed. The cock will commence the initial nest-building with the hen adding the finishing touches.

BREEDING SEASON

The normal breeding season for birds is the spring, when the hours of daylight are increasing. Most species will lay two or more clutches in a season, but more than three is not recommended as it will greatly strain the hen in particular. Species such as Zebras and many birds bred indoors are capable of breeding into and through the winter because artificial daylight and regulated heat are possible. However, it is open to debate whether the chicks produced at this time are as vigorous; certainly late aviary breeding is less productive as the availability of livefood and greenfood recedes

One of the more uncommon firefinches in aviculture is the Dark Firefinch, *Lagonosticta rubricata.*

The open nest is acceptable to some finch pairs, while others will prefer a covered enclosure.

in the autumn. Further, sudden frosts are possible, depending on where you live, and even if this does not kill the chicks, it will certainly retard their growth, as more protein and fats will be used purely to insulate rather than to build body.

EGGLAYING

Finches are variable in the number of eggs they lay, but a general indication would be three to four.

Incubation lasts from 12 to 14 days, while the young will leave the nest in 13 to 16 days, the exceptions being in the case of the Weaver Finches which fledge in 18 to 21 days. Incubation may be carried out almost exclusively by the hen, this being true of buntings and finches, or it may be shared, as in the case of the Weaver Finches. Incubation may commence with the last egg, but may also start with the second egg laid. The fact that a hen is "sitting" does not always mean she has actually commenced laying, but this will normally follow shortly after. The eggs of finches may be of various colors and may or may not be marked with blotches or spots—the exception being the Weaver Finches who all lay white eggs.

REARING CHICKS

Assuming all has gone well with the laying and incubation, during the crucial first few days of their lives the chicks will receive what is termed "crop milk" from the hen. The quality of this will be a direct reflection of the hen's diet. If this is lacking then the chicks will suffer as a result or the hen may even stop feeding them. One of the commercial canary or finch rearing

softfoods should be supplied twice a day: once early in the

Like many finch species, the Purple Grenadier Waxbill, *Uraeginthus ianthinogaster*, becomes highly insectivorous when breeding.

morning and again the early evening, but while it is still light. This can be moistened into a paste by the addition of milk or carrot juice and supplemented with wheat germ, yeast, and cod liver oil. Dried livefood can be added and the whole will make a really strong body-building mix for the hen to feed to her chicks.

At this time, supply germinated seeds and soaked millet sprays, as well as plenty of greenfood. Do not forget to keep up a high ration of calcium. Initially it was required by the hen to form good eggshell, now it is needed so the chicks will develop strong bone and the hen also has a need to keep her vigor up.

After fledging, the chicks will still be fed by the cock for another 10 to 18 days, but as soon as you see the chicks are able to feed themselves, then they should be removed, as they are in danger of being attacked by the parents, especially the cock. They should be placed in a stock cage and seed placed both in pots or hoppers and on the cage floor until they are familiar with eating from pots. Continue to feed them with softfood and all the other varieties of food, as you want strong, healthy birds. Place the cage perches somewhat lower for these youngsters. It is a good idea to use branches (replaced every day or two) of fruit trees for perches as these will offer a range of thickness for the perching chicks, and this will be good exercise for their feet. If standard dwelling is used it should be roughened, not smooth, and on no account use plastic perches.

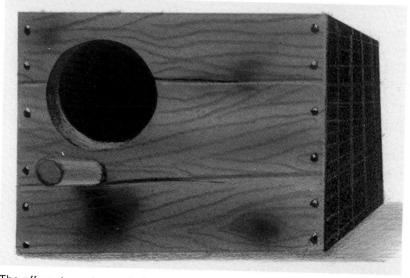

The off-center entrance hole serves to provide more privacy than do other nest box designs.

FOSTER PARENTS

There are occasions when foster parents are needed. A hen may abandon her eggs, she may die, or she may lay a second round of eggs while young chicks are in the nest, in which case she might throw the chicks out. Again, if you have successfully bred with non-prolific species you may wish to have a second clutch of eggs underway as quickly as possible. In each of these cases, a species such as the Bengalese can be used as a foster.

Of course, the foster parents must be at a comparable state of breeding, so you are advised to have a number of fosters at differing stages of egg and chick rearing, so that the intended foster chicks can be placed

Finch nest box of the half-open design—some finch pairs will prefer the larger entrance. The sliding top simplifies nest inspection, and the full-length shelf-perch is as simple to install as any.

Zebra Finch chicks in their nest; these two appear to be the Pied variety.

with similar staged eggs or chicks. Simply mark the eggs to be fostered with a felt tip pen, remove one or more of the foster hen's eggs and the Bengalese will incubate the eggs and rear the chicks on her own. The eggs are marked so that if the hen lays further eggs you know which to remove. I do not recommend that fostering become a regular procedure because it is important that you know the true parents are capable of rearing their own young; fostering, like many other aspects of aviculture, should be viewed as just another tool at your disposal to aid your breeding; it should not become the "norm".

IDENTIFICATION

It is obviously essential that you are able to identify the various birds in your collection. Once chicks have molted out you will be hard-pressed to know the parents from the yearlings. Identification is facilitated by the use of various rings. These may be metal (aluminum) or plastic and they may be either open or closed. Plastic rings come in an assortment of colors and may be two-tone or single color, numbered or not. They are available from certain pet stores, specialist clubs or from the manufacturers who advertise in the avicultural press. When ordering, state the species they are for. Closed rings are a permanent source of identification while open rings are easily removed, and thus act as temporary markings easily spotted in the aviary. Ringing is not the ideal means of permanent identification

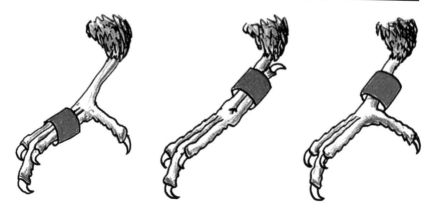

Above: Closed banding is accomplished by first pulling the band over the three forward toes, up onto the leg and the hind toe, and then extracting the hind toe from the band (with a toothpick or something similar).
Below: A pair of Green Twinspots, *Mandingoa nitidula.*

simply because birds can get themselves caught up on the rings, but it is the best form we have at this time.

Rings should be placed on the chicks when they are about seven to ten days old. If they are too loose, try then to fit them one or two days later. They must never be over-tight, as this could result in the loss of a foot. Placing rings on is simply a case of sliding one over the front three toes and gently, with the aid of a pointed matchstick, easing the ring up the leg and over the rear toe. Have a breeder demonstrate this for you.

HAND-REARING

Finches, because of their small size, are not the easiest birds to hand-rear. This obviously depends on the age at which this might become necessary. You are advised to purchase a hand-rearing syringe or crop feeder so that you have it available when required. The feeder is filled with a semi-liquid food, made by using boiling water and allowing it to cool to body temperature after mixing, and this is inserted into the waiting bird's crop. Before doing so, tap the syringe while it is held vertically; this will send any air to the top and this should be expelled. It is better to feed little and often than risk choking the chick with excess. Feeding must be done about every hour or two throughout the day and only leave a gap of about four hours overnight. It is very hard work, but the resulting chicks will become very tame birds.

Woven wicker nests are designed to be hung on the wire or wall of a cage or flight.

Health Matters

It is always better to prevent illness than to cure it, and this is a very practical attitude to adopt in the case of finches in particular. Unlike larger birds, where you have a reasonable time period in which to effect a diagnosis and apply treatment, finches can be unwell in one hour and dead in the next; such is the pace of their metabolism. Further, the *average* veterinarian has only limited knowledge of avian disorders, though in recent years the number who have taken an interest in birds has grown considerably. Thus you may well be the first and last line of defense, as it were, for your birds.

It is probable that the two major reasons for avian illnesses are absence of hygiene on the one hand, and incorrect nutrition on the other. Overcrowding, lack of ventilation, and incorrect acclimatization and quarantine (in your aviaries), are other sources of problems. Often, sudden noises can stress a bird so much that it can quite literally die of fright, and if not, then the stress may well reduce its ability to overcome a minor disorder to the degree that this becomes a major problem. In actual fact, when you catalogue the potential problems, it is almost amazing that we are able to keep them alive at all! Indeed, in many species we are unable to do exactly that, while many of today's popular birds were once considered "difficult", and it is only

In this illustration of a perched goldfinch, the bones of wings and legs have been rendered in blue, while the skull and the rest of the skeleton are depicted in yellow.

by recognizing these straightforward problems that major epidemics in our aviaries are avoided.

Feeding utensils must be thoroughly washed in hot water, and they should be replaced periodically—and most certainly if any cracks appear in them or if they get chipped. Cages should be cleaned at least once per week, as should aviaries. Perches should not be kept for months and months, but should be renewed on a regular basis. By always having a surplus of stock and breeder cages, you are always able to disinfect and, by rotation, leave cages unused for a minimum of three weeks. It is very easy to fall into the trap of handling a number of birds without washing our hands after each bird—we all do it, but it is another way of spreading disease.

It obviously pays to take a close look at our birds every day, and if the collection grows so large that we are unable to do so, then either an extra helper is needed or the collection needs to be reduced. This is simple sound husbandry. If you are at all unsure about the way a bird is looking then catch it, isolate it, and give it warmth. Thinking about it overnight on the grounds that "I will see how it looks tomorrow," could just be fatal to it.

If a number of birds are kept, then the acquisition of a hospital cage is a sound investment. There are numerous models, but the simplest, yet very effective, one is that in which a heat lamp (infrared) is attached to

The Gray Singing Finch, *Serinus leucopygius*—a close relative of the canary, is appreciated for its song.

a stock cage. The lamp is at one end so that the bird can move into or away from the heat as required. Water must always be available and medications can be placed into this. The heat creates thirst and thus the medicine is taken. Heat alone can work miracles in reviving a bird, but remember, it must then be carefully acclimatized back to its cage or aviary temperature. Those birdkeepers who have a steady turnover in birds are obviously more at risk to illness in their stock than are those whose collection is only added to infrequently. The following are the problems one is more likely to come up against. Should your bird die, then a postmortem, though expensive in relation to the bird's cost, is often

The Madagascar Weaver, *Foudia madagascariensis*, male and female.

worthwhile as it might pinpoint a source which you had overlooked.

Airsac Mite This respiratory ailment is caused by the mite *Sternostoma tracheacolum* and affects canaries,

Male Red-cheeked Cordon Bleu,
Uraeginthus bengalus.

Gouldian Finches and other birds, including the budgerigar. Loss of voice is accompanied by coughing, wheezing, and gasping for breath—in turn this creates drowsiness due to lack of sleep. Infected birds may pass on the mites via food to chicks.

Treatment is by means of mixing the insecticide carbaryl with seeds coated with cod liver oil or similar. Consult your veterinarian for dosage, as the insecticide is also fatal to birds if in excess.

Beaks Occasionally a beak (or claws) may become overgrown. In such cases the bird should be held firmly, yet gently, and the excess trimmed back with nail clippers. Do not cut into the "quick" which is the blood vessel; too little is better than too much.

Dead-in-Shell Various causes are given for this problem, including lack of humidity. However, it is more likely that a mineral or vitamin deficiency is the major problem, and due to this the egg is unable to lose water, the chick in effect drowning. It is not known if there is a genetic base to the problem, so do not breed hens who show an incidence of it on more than one occasion—especially if your other birds do not have this problem with eggs.

Diarrhea This can be caused by many things and may itself be symptomatic of many disorders. Isolate the bird, reduce the greenfood part of the diet and treat with aureomycin or terramycin for about five days under veterinary instruction. Because of the potential risk of spreading the condition—and what it might be symptomatic of—bad cases should be kept in isolation for some time, and until microscopic analysis of the feces has been made.

Eggbinding This distressing condition for a hen is the result of incorrect feeding prior to egglaying,

Closely related to the blue waxbills is the larger Violet-eared Waxbill, *Uraeginthus granatina*.

overweight, and lack of essential minerals, such as calcium. The eggshell is not correctly formed and becomes soft; when the hen contracts to expel the egg it "gives" and thus does not move down the oviduct.

Alternatively, if she is overweight her muscles do not provide sufficient grip to push the egg towards her vent. Unless the problem egg is released quickly, the hen will most likely die through overexertion. The standard cure is to place the hen (handle with great care) in a warm environment where the temperature is about 29°C (85°F). Call your veterinarian, as surgical removal may be required. Do not breed such a hen another time in that season as she must be fully fit before being used again. If she has already laid eggs then foster these if possible.

Eye Problems These may simply be caused by foreign bodies setting up an irritation in the eye, or they may be symptoms of other more serious diseases. For minor problems, gentle bathing in a mild saline solution, or treatment with eye ointment under veterinary instruction will usually clear matters up. If the bird does not respond quickly to such treatment, then a more serious problem is indicated.

Feather Plucking Sometimes a hen will habitually pluck the feathers of her chicks and if carried to excess this can cause lasting damage to the plumage. Such hens are best not used in future breeding. At the time, the answer is to remove chicks to a foster parent or handrear them. Minor plucking of feathers is not unusual. In adults, feather plucking indicates an incorrect diet, lack of exercise or stress, and is very difficult to overcome. Such birds, if in cages, should be given to someone who has an aviary.

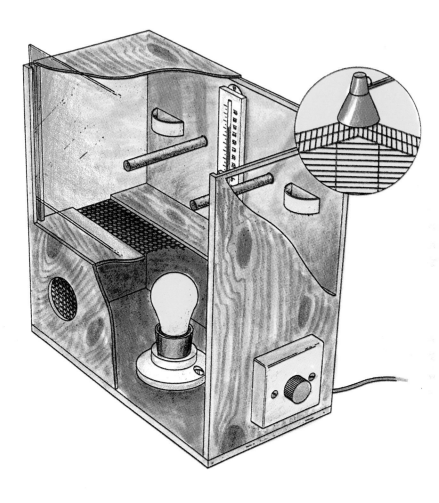

Ill birds benefit from warmth, so hospital cages have been constructed. The transparent front panel prevents heat from escaping. In this instance, a light bulb below a grid supplies the heat. A thermometer and a control help to keep the temperature within a suitable range. Lacking such a cage, similar results may be produced by placing a lamp above a wire cage, as the inset shows.

Intestinal Worms The worms which may affect birds are tapeworm, roundworm, and thread worms. In each case, the symptoms are a general lack of vigor and loss of weight. Aviary birds are more susceptible than are cage birds, as often the worms are passed to aviary birds via the droppings of wild birds or they are ingested via insects which, in some cases, are intermediate hosts of the worms. Treatment should follow microscopic confirmation of their presence and species, but treatment of choice is usually the drug piperazine adipate. Aviaries with concrete floors should be blowtorched to eradicate the worms and eggs, while soiled aviaries should be periodically left free of birds and treated with insecticides—thus a spare aviary for rotation of use is always advisable.

Parasites (External) The most common external parasites on cage birds are various species of mites *Dermanyssus sp.)* and lice *(Ornithonyssus* and *Liponyssus sp.).* The former live away from the host and are more difficult to eradicate, whereas the latter species can live and breed on the host, so are more easily treated. Red mites suck the blood of the host and then return to crevices in the woodwork. Treatment of the birds is of secondary importance to destroying the hiding places of these mites, for unless this is done, they will merely reinfest your birds again. Heavy infestations will severely debilitate a bird, and hens may abandon chicks in

Zebra Finch show cage containing a pair of Chestnut-flanked Whites. The carrying case, designed to facilitate transporting birds to shows, can accommodate three such cages.

The Baya Weaver, *Ploceus phillipinus*, a cock in breeding plumage.

Treat with a proprietary acaricide after thorough cleaning and burning of all potentially infested materials. Double check all dark corners and repaint. It is better that the aviary be vacated if heavy infestation is obvious. The problem known as *scalyface* and *scalyleg* are also caused by arachnids and their treatment is straightforward by use of one of many acaricides according to the manufacturer's instructions.

Wounds Happily, wounds are not a major problem in finches and minor ones will quickly heal. They can be wiped with a mild saline solution or antiseptic. In more serious cases, the bird should be immobilized by being wrapped in cloth and taken promptly to your veterinarian.

such circumstances. The chicks, likewise, will suffer badly. Often, secondary worm and lice infestation is likely, as well as infections resulting from the scratching and feather plucking by the birds.

The Golden Sparrow, *Auripasser luteus*, is one of a number of African finch species with a conspicuous amount of yellow in the plumage.

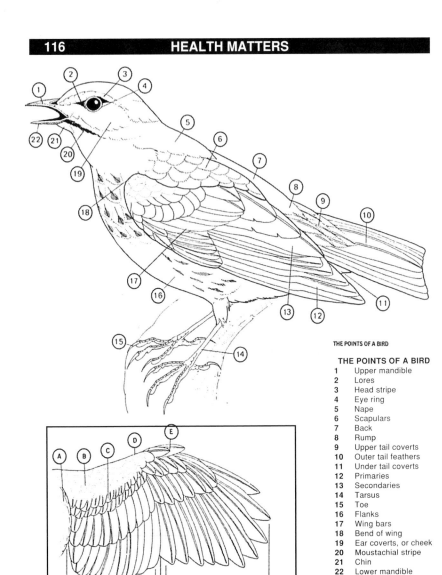

THE POINTS OF A BIRD

THE POINTS OF A BIRD

1	Upper mandible
2	Lores
3	Head stripe
4	Eye ring
5	Nape
6	Scapulars
7	Back
8	Rump
9	Upper tail coverts
10	Outer tail feathers
11	Under tail coverts
12	Primaries
13	Secondaries
14	Tarsus
15	Toe
16	Flanks
17	Wing bars
18	Bend of wing
19	Ear coverts, or cheek
20	Moustachial stripe
21	Chin
22	Lower mandible

THE POINTS OF A WING

A	Axillaries
B	Wing coverts
C	Wing linings
D	Fore-edge of wing
E	Thumb pinion
F	Secondaries
G	Rear edge of wing
H	Primaries

TOPOGRAPHY OF A FINCH-LIKE BIRD

Finch Species

It was mentioned in the introduction that an understanding of how birds are classified scientifically will be of great help to any aviculturist. The reason for this is apparent if one looks at dealer listings. For example, one might see an advertisement in which Crimson Finches are offered for sale, but unless you are familiar with the usual prices of birds there would be no way of knowing whether it was the neotropical bunting, *Rhodospingus cruentus* or the Australian Grass Finch, *Neochmia phaeton* that was on offer. Likewise, the Red Avadavat is also known as the Red Munia or Tiger Finch. Indeed, nearly all finches have two or more names which are referred to as common names. This situation is obviously unacceptable to those who have a need to precisely define what species of bird, or indeed any animal, is under discussion.

Carolus Linnaeus established the nomenclatural system used by zoologists to distinguish animal species.

The Crimson Finch, *Neochmia phaeton*, a male.

The system by which this is achieved was devised by a Swedish naturalist, Carolus Linnaeus, whose work, *Systema Naturae*, published in 1758, forms the basis of modern taxonomy or classification. The system is known as the binomial system of nomenclature, and in it every plant and animal is given a double name which is unique to it. By a series of divisions, all animals are placed into groups based on similarities. The higher

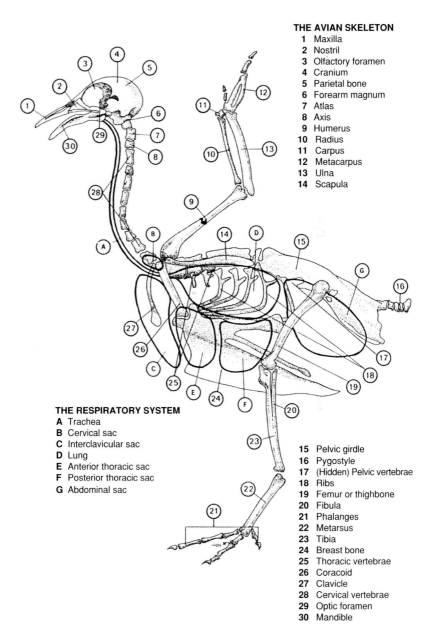

THE AVIAN SKELETON
1 Maxilla
2 Nostril
3 Olfactory foramen
4 Cranium
5 Parietal bone
6 Forearm magnum
7 Atlas
8 Axis
9 Humerus
10 Radius
11 Carpus
12 Metacarpus
13 Ulna
14 Scapula

THE RESPIRATORY SYSTEM
A Trachea
B Cervical sac
C Interclavicular sac
D Lung
E Anterior thoracic sac
F Posterior thoracic sac
G Abdominal sac

15 Pelvic girdle
16 Pygostyle
17 (Hidden) Pelvic vertebrae
18 Ribs
19 Femur or thighbone
20 Fibula
21 Phalanges
22 Metarsus
23 Tibia
24 Breast bone
25 Thoracic vertebrae
26 Coracoid
27 Clavicle
28 Cervical vertebrae
29 Optic foramen
30 Mandible

ANATOMY OF A FINCH-LIKE BIRD

In European Bullfinches, *Pyrrhula pyrrhula*, the sexes are easily distinguished.

the group, the more general are the affinities, the lower the group, the more closely related the animals are—in effect you have a triangle in which life itself forms the apex and all the species are placed on the bottom line.

All birds belong to the class Aves and this is divided into 27 orders, such as the parrots (psittaciformes), birds of prey (falconiformes), and so on. The finches are within the order known as Passeriformes, the perching birds. There are about 4,000 birds in this group, which comprises about half of all birds. Orders are divided into many families, and we are concerned with just four of these. Families are divided into numerous genera (singular genus) and by this stage the birds are very similar in many anatomical features. In order to distinguish differing members of the same genus, each bird is given its own name, and when this is used in conjunction with the generic name, then the bird is a recognized species. Often, there are regional races of the same species and these are distinguished by being given a third name thus forming a trinomial. When this happens, the originally identified bird repeats its specific or trivial name and is then known as the nominate race, being an example of its type.

A Red-eared Waxbill, *Estrilda trogodytes*, carrying a blade of grass for courtship.

It is often practical to include extra divisions within the system so that one will find, in most cases, there are suborders, subfamilies, and so on. Obviously, the system is being continually revised in the light of increased knowledge of groups and species and this results in birds being moved from one genus, or even family, to another.

Linnaeus decided to use a "dead" language for the system as this would be more acceptable to all nations. Further, as Latin was the language used at that time for scholars, it was the obvious choice. Greek and French are now also seen within scientific names. It is customary to write scientific names in italics. This applies to the genus and trivial names only. The genus always commences with a capital letter and the trivial name with a lowercase one. The genus may be shortened to its initial letter, or omitted altogether, after its first usage in text provided one does not then discuss another genus. The name often appearing after a species is the name of the person who originally named that species and if the bird has since been placed in a differing genus, then the person's name is placed in parentheses.

When visiting foreign countries, the names of birds in zoos and similar places will appear both in the vernacular and in the scientific language. This is true of books, magazines and most printed references to birds; thus knowledge of the system is beneficial.

The four families we

Mutual preening in the Gold-breasted Waxbill, *Amandava subflava*.

are interested in are dealt with in rotation and contain some 975 species, the vast majority of which are not commonly found in aviculture. I have chosen not to include the large grosbeaks and cardinals in the text simply because these would have no place in a mixed collection of smaller finches. Those species covered are therefore the birds which the average person would, on seeing them, consider to be "finches." A representative selection of birds is described from each family and all of them are available to birdkeepers. They range from the inexpensive to the very costly.

Fortunately, a costly finch would only equate to a relatively inexpensive parrot, so we are lucky in this respect, but finches are more delicate, so actual comparisons are possibly misleading; nonetheless, one can establish a mixed collection of finches for a fraction of the cost of a mixed group of parrots or softbilled birds.

The classification used in this text is that of *A Complete Checklist of the Birds in the World.*

FAMILY EMBERIZIDAE

This is a multifarious collection of birds which range in size from the tiny grassquits of the neotropics to the large cardinals of North and South America. It also contains the buntings of the Old World and their New World equivalents, together with numerous other finchlike species. Over the years, members of the family have been included in other families or given their own family status, and no doubt there will be much revision of the group in the future, given the diversity of forms found within the present family. As a whole, the group is not especially popular in aviculture, though certain species will appear in most collections over the years. One of the reasons for many people not keeping them is a simple case of its being either illegal to do so or that supplies are rarely available. For example, the much-prized Virginia cardinal, together with numerous most beautiful American buntings, cannot be kept by American birdkeepers because keeping any species that is native to the U.S.A. is illegal. These birds are available,

The male Virginia Cardinal, *Cardinalis cardinalis*, is one of the most conspicuous passerines in Eastern North America.

The Yellow-rumped Seedeater, *Serinus atrogularis*, is typical of a number of African species that are occasionally imported.

Grassquit) were commonly imported into the U.S.A. and Europe, but their export is now banned so availability is greatly reduced. The import ban in Australia likewise restricts Australian fanciers from most of the popular Emberizids and it is illegal for most Europeans to keep wild- caught members of this family that are native to their country. Thus, one is left with only neotropical species and those of Africa, Asia, and elsewhere, many of which are not especially colorful, therefore unappealing, to birdkeepers. To make matters worse the number of potential pairs imported is low as often there is either a shortage of cocks or hens.

however, to non-Americans because their range often extends to Mexico where they are caught.

Many years ago, species such as the Cuban Finch (Cuban

Most members of the group are ground feeders and when

rearing young will require a considerable increase in their daily livefood supply. Incubation is by the hen, though the cock will sit occasionally when the hen is away from the nest. Generally, members of this family are better housed and bred as individual pairs, rather than in mixed collections, as they tend to be aggressive towards other birds at this time. This is especially true if they are with their own kind or with closely related species, where fighting will be of a very serious nature. Out of the breeding season most are quite peaceful but as they are self-assertive birds, should not be placed with timid or very small species, such as waxbills, who will be nervous at their presence. All Emberizids tend to be

The House Finch, *Carpodacus mexicanus.*

in the mid price range of finches, while the reduced availability of certain species will be reflected in quite high prices.

In the following text, color descriptions are minimal, being restricted to the most obvious features, the excellent photos in this book imparting far better images than can words. A number of the birds are treated individually, whereas others are dealt with in a more collective way, which enables a greater number of species to be covered.

Blackcrested Finch
Lophospingus pusillus
13cm (5 in.)

This bird is often called a Pygmy Cardinal due to its resemblance in shape, to the Green Cardinal. Although its colors are simple—shades of gray and white with a black crest on its head—it is nonetheless a pleasing bird. Formerly imported into Europe in quite large numbers, and somewhat less so into the U.S.A., it is rather aggressive, so must be in the company of birds that can stand up for themselves. When available it is rather expensive, but it is an interesting addition to a collection.

Distribution S. Bolivia, Paraguay, and Argentina.

Hen Similar to cock but duller and lacking the black throat spot.

Breeding These birds will accept various types of nestboxes, so nest pans or baskets should be tried. The clutch size is two or three greeny-gray eggs which are incubated for about 12 days. Fledging is likewise at about 12 days. Weaning is after a further 25-30 days and it is advisable to remove chicks as soon as possible so they are not subject to attacks from the cock.

Saffron Finch *Sicalis flaveola* 14cm (5 1/2 in.)

This is a very popular bird and as such is one of the less expensive Emberizids. The males are a most attractive golden yellow and have

The several forms of the Saffron Finch, *Sicalis flaveola*, are widely distributed throughout South America.

a pleasing, if not brilliant, song. Once acclimatized they are very hardy birds and can cope with northern winters, providing they have access to well-insulated shelters.

They must be treated very much on an individual pair basis in mixed collections, some being very tolerant, others less so, of other species. They are not likely to attack small finches but they intimidate them with their presence, so much depends on the aviary size. Well

Saffron Finch, *Sicalis flaveola*.

recommended.

Distribution Colombia, south through Venezuela, Peru, Brazil, Uruguay, Paraguay, and Argentina.

Hen Very pale by comparison to the cock, thus easily

recognized. Much more streaking of yellowish-brown on the body.

Breeding Budgerigar nestbox, either with hole or half- open will be accepted in which the hen will build a crude nest. Clutch size two to five eggs which are white mottled with blue-brown-black spots. Incubation 12-14 days. Fledging is after 14-17 days, after which the cock will feed the chicks for a further 10-14 days. Remove chicks at earliest opportunity. These finches will take a standard budgie seed mixture or one for finches. Will cage breed in suitable size. There are 12 species in the genus, all basically yellow birds, and there are four subspecies of the Saffron Finch, the nominate race being that generally imported.

GRASSQUITS AND SEEDEATERS

These small finches are contained in a number of genera and range from the very plain to very attractive. Availability of the grassquits has dramatically reduced over the years, while the seedeaters are sporadic in supply, and often of unknown species—few being kept by aviculturists, so information is somewhat sparse. Both groups are hardy and aggressive little birds that will quickly bully other finches, so need to be kept in mixed aviaries with the likes of weavers or Java Sparrows, who can give as good as they get when the feathers start flying!

The Jacarini finch (Blueblack Grassquit), *Volatinia jacarina*, is less aggressive with unrelated species than are other grassquits. It

Cuban Finch, *Tiaris canora.*

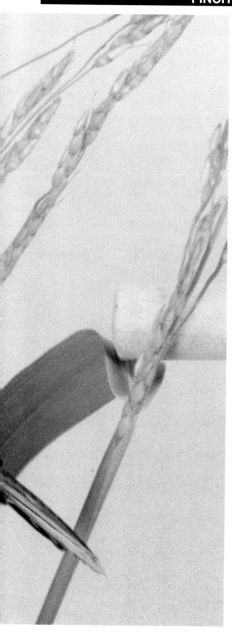

is predominantly a black finch, and has a characteristic jumping action when displaying to females. The Cuban Finch (Grassquit), *Tiaris canora*, was once bred in large numbers in Europe, but stocks have dwindled since the Cuban ban on exports. It will be very costly if you see a pair for sale. They are pretty little birds in which the black and yellow of the head is the striking feature. Females are much duller. Similar and more readily available will be the Olive Finch (Yellow-faced Grassquit), *T.olivacea*, as the distribution of this bird includes Mexico and Central America. Size of the species mentioned here is 10cm (4 in.) or slightly larger.

The seedeaters have pleasant songs but are usually rather lacking

Olive Finch, *Tiaris olivacea*. The female is similarly colored, but duller.

in color. They are neotropical in distribution and quite hardy once acclimatized. Nestcups and baskets should be supplied for these birds, both groups, and again livefood is needed during the breeding season. The most likely seedeaters to be available will be members of the genus *Sporophila*, which contains some 32 species.

One interesting seedeater is the Parrotbilled, which, as its name suggests, has a curved parrotlike beak. In others the bills are somewhat like those of grosbeaks in shape and proportion to the head.

New World Buntings

This group of six species in the genus *Passerina* are not true buntings. They are, however, among the most desirable of all finches of the Americas. Five species are well-known to aviculture, the Rosita (Rose-bellied) being unknown and on which one can find no reference in avicultural books. These birds are not available as freely as in past years and their price has climbed steadily. Most certainly they will become extremely expensive in future years as breeding success with them is minimal and very much needed. This is partly because of their need for an insectivorous diet, but also because they are shy, retiring birds that need plenty of cover in which to nest, and as little disturbance as possible. Of course, only the Rainbow Bunting (Orange-breasted), may be kept by American breeders as the other four species are all native to the U.S.A.

The color of these birds is quite spectacular, combining blue, yellow, and green in the rainbow, the addition of reds in the painted, while the Indigo and Lazuli are mainly blue with brown; the versicolor (varied) combines blue, red, browns, and black. The Indigo has the widest distribution, extending from southern Canada down to Venezuela, also Jamaica.

These are not really hardy birds and are better accommodated in heated quarters during the winters of northern U.S.A. and Europe. Each species will nest in thick shrubs a few feet above ground level and should be supplied with nesting material and even a small open box which they may use. Clutch size is two

Orange-breasted Bunting pair, *Passerina leclancheri.* Among the *Passerina* buntings, females are significantly less colorful.

The Indigo Bunting, *Passerina cyanea*, will choose a dense thicket for a nesting site.

round. Do not keep more than one per aviary, and inclusion in a mixed aviary is not recommended if breeding is to be attempted—which should be if a pair can be acquired. The five species in aviculture are:

INDIGO BUNTING
Passerina cyanea 13cm (5 in.)

Hens duller than cock, but the cock's color resembles that of hen out of breeding season.

LAZULI BUNTING *P. amoena* 12cm (4 3/4 in.)
Hen dull version of cock.

VERSICOLOR (VARIED) BUNTING *P. versicolor* 12cm (4 3/4 in.)
Hen dull colors.

PAINTED BUNTING *P. ciris* 13cm (5 in.)
Hen duller version of cock and with no blue

to four and incubation will last 11 to 13 days. Fledging is about 10 to 13 days, after which parents will feed the youngsters, the hen ceasing to do so when she lays a second

The Lazuli Bunting, *Passerina amoena*, (left) and the Versicolor Bunting, *Passerina versicolor*, (right) occur principally in the western and southwestern parts of the United States and in Mexico.

Upper pair, Green-backed Twinspots; lower pair, Peter's Twinspots.

(1) Gray Singing Finch; Alario Finches: female (2); male (3).

Orange-breasted Bunting, *Passerina leclancheri.*

on head; red is replaced with off-yellow.

RAINBOW (ORANGE-BREASTED) BUNTING *P. leclancheri* 13cm (5 in.)

Hen very dull compared to cock, mainly olive green with dull yellow underparts.

FAMILY FRINGILLIDAE

This family contains 121 species in 19 genera, and is divided into two subfamilies. The chaffinches, two species, and the single brambling species comprise the subfamily Fringillidae, and the remaining species are all contained in the subfamily Carduelinae. In actual fact, in terms of finchlike birds in aviculture, few members of this family are kept, though one member is probably the most well-known of all finches—the

The Chaffinch, *Fringilla coelebs*, is the best known representative of the "true finches."

Brambling, *Fringilla montifringilla,* a male.

canary. We are only concerned with the Carduelinae who have a wide distribution that is global except for Madagascar and Australia, where certain species are established in the wild, but are introduced and not native. Males of this family feed the incubating hen and will occasionally take a turn themselves at setting. A number breed as pairs through many form colonies of varying numbers. Nests are tidy and cupshaped, built by the hen with cocks supplying the labor of carrying a few pieces of material! The cocks are famed for their

Brambling, *Fringilla montifringilla*, female.

Eurasian Linnet, *Acanthis cannabina*.

The Linnet has a considerable reputation as a songster.

melodious song, and for this reason alone, a number of not especially attractive species are usually included in a mixed collection. Bullfinches, Goldfinches and Linnets are all used for crossing to the canary, the resulting offspring being superb songsters invariably superior to either parent. In Europe, the breeding of such birds is very much a specialized business with a strong following. Access to many European species is very restricted for Americans but birds such as the European goldfinch are much prized by Americans, justifiably, given the beauty of these birds.

Australians have no access to the true finches other than those already within the country before import bans were imposed. As a result, stocks are falling and some species will no doubt vanish due to insufficient breeding pairs being available. Prices of foreign finches are thus always increasing, and it is to the Australians' credit that they have retained a number of species as long as they have. As with British breeders of Australian species, the Australians have shown what can be achieved against the odds.

As the canary is such a well-known bird in captivity, it is not included in this text, but beginners are certainly recommended to include these beautiful birds within their initial collections, both for their color and song. They are also prolific breeders, hardy and thus ideal as introductions to practical finch breeding.

Eurasian Bullfinch, *Pyrrhula pyrrhula*. This species has been appreciated by fanciers for its color and form; farmers, on the other hand, complain about its consumption of buds and fruits.

The hen Eurasian Bullfinch, *Pyrrhula pyrrhula,* is marked like the male but with different colors.

The European Goldfinch, *Carduelis carduelis,* a male.

Gray Singing Finch, *Serinus leucopygius.*

Gray Singing Finch (White-Rumped Seedeater) *Serinus leucopygius* 10cm (4 in.)

This little songster has always been, and remains, a popular aviary bird and it is its magnificent voice rather than its dull gray and white appearance that is its great virtue. It is also quite hardy, a reliable breeder and a tough little character that will more than hold its own against larger tough boys such as Java sparrows, Weavers, or Grassquits. Gray Singers are remarkably long-lived for such little birds and 15 to 20 years is by no means exceptional. They can become very tame. They build neat nests which they will defend very strongly. They are relatively inexpensive to buy and most breeders of mixed collections find their chirpy and lively dispositions easily outweigh their somewhat bland appearance.

Distribution Senegal, Chad, Ethiopia, Sudan, and Nigeria.

Hen Similar to the cock; to sex, separate them and the cock is usually the one who will sing nonstop.

Breeding Various nestboxes will be used; nestpans, baskets or open boxes, which are best placed among foliage. Clutch size three to four which may be bluish, greenish or just white—with dark spots. Incubation 12 to 14 days. Fledging 12 to 14 days. Unless a second clutch is laid the chicks are usually safe with their parents after fledging.

The Green Singing Finch (Yellow-fronted Canary), *S. mozambicus*, which is slightly larger, is much more attractive, though slightly less able in the singing department, but is still superb. This little green and yellow bird will be about the same price as the gray and possibly more plentiful. The hen is paler than the cock.

Other members of the genus *Serinus* that are sometimes on offer will be the St. Helena Seedeater (Yellow Canary), *S.flaviventris*, which is similar to the Green Singer, the Blackthroated Canary (Yellow-Rumped Seedeater), *S.atrogularis* and the Cape Canary (Yellow-Crowned), *S.canicollis*. Each of these are variations on the singing finch theme. In all, there are 32 species within this genus.

European Goldfinch, *Carduelis carduelis*. Appealing both for its color and its song, this species has long been one of the most popular cage birds in Europe. A further point of interest has been that it will hybridize with canaries.

Siskins, Goldfinches and Greenfinches Genus
Carduelis

This genus contains 24 species and includes a number of birds that are popular in European aviaries. One of these, the Hooded Siskin (Red), *Carduelis cucullata*, is especially known to color canary breeders, as it was used to introduce the red factor. It is a beautiful and now much-prized aviary bird that is rarely available due to the ban on its export from its main homeland of Venezuela. With black on its head and red body it is most attractive and quite hardy once acclimatized, but expensive even if you have the opportunity of a pair. Size is four and a half inches. Niger is an important seed within its diet, nest is cupshaped.

Hooded Siskin, *Carduelis cucullata*, male.

Hooded Siskin, *Carduelis cucullata*, female.

There are other siskins offered from time to time and though not as colorful as the hooded, nonetheless make intersting aviary occupants of good song. In all cases both niger and ample greenfood is important.

European Goldfinch
Carduelis carduelis
13cm (5 in.)
There are 12 subspecies of this, the most colorful of European finches. These are hardy birds and reliable breeders which can be cage bred. The clutch size

is three to five eggs, incubated by the female. Normal finch diet is required with increased amounts of canary seed plus a little rape and linseed—of course, ample greenfood and insectivorous food during breeding season. The Goldfinch, together with the Greenfinch and Sparrows, were introduced into Australia where they quickly established themselves. Thus the first two named are popular aviary birds "down under."

The most attractive black and yellow coloring of the American Goldfinch, *C.tristis*, makes it desirable, but it is seldom available, and illegal to American breeders. The Darkbacked Goldfinch, *C.psaltia*, is sometimes also available in Europe.

The markings of the goldfinch parent are clearly visible in this
European Goldfinch x canary hybrid.

The Greenfinches of this family are less colorful than the Goldfinches, being a mixture of green, yellow and brown. Nor are these birds especially good singers, and as they can be rather aggressive during the breeding season these various factors restrict their popularity to specialist breeders.

Rosefinches Genus
Carpodacus

There are 21 species of Rosefinch, most of which are found in Asia and China; others are found in the U.S.A., Canada, and Mexico. When newly purchased they exhibit an attractive rose-colored hue on their feathers, but this fades, thus rendering them less colorful. It would appear that color feeding them with canary food retards, but does not stop, this loss of color in captivity. They are not especially cheap birds to buy. Size is variable around five and a half inches, and as they can be aggressive are best housed with species that are not easily intimidated. Unlikely to appeal to those just beginning in aviculture.

Green Singing Finch, *Serinus mozambicus.*

Upper bird, *Erythrura psittacea;* lower bird, *Erythrura prasina.*

Scarlet Rosefinch, *Erythrina erythrina,* male and female.

Wild-caught male Zebra Finch, *Poephila guttata guttata*.

The House Finch, *Carpodacus mexicanus*, is an example of a number of finch species that have plainly colored bodies and a variable amount of reddish color extending from the head.

Bullfinches Genus
Pyrrhula

Of the six bullfinch species it the various subspecies of the nominate race that are kept in aviculture. The British Bullfinch, *P. pileata*, with its black head and chestnut body is most appealing and somewhat unusual in shape, the head seemingly sitting directly on the shoulders. These birds pair for life and require a diet in which berries figure strongly. The hens build neat nests but may as easily lay the eggs on the aviary floor as in the nest! Hens are usually in short supply. The Siberian, Chinese (Beavan's) and Japanese Bullfinches are all most attractive, having much gray on the bodies contrasted with either orange, rose, black, and white—depending on the species. Prices are very variable reflecting availability, or lack of it.

In concluding this review of the Embrizids, it cannot be overstressed, and this applies to nearly all finchlike birds, that seed should form only part of the diet of your birds; it is a convenient food but is not a complete diet and greenfood and livefood must be available throughout the year and in large quantities during breeding periods.

An unpainted show cage for finches, showing details of construction for the water pot and the door.

Show cage containing a Chestnut-flanked White Zebra Finch pair.

Of the domesticated Bengalese Finch varieties, the Self Chocolate is probably closest to the appearance of the ancestral form.

FAMILY ESTRILDIDAE

Although not the largest of the finchlike bird families, the birds of this group include more popular cage and aviary birds than any other family. There are some 131 species in 28 genera and all are found in the Old World, the vast majority—over half of them—being native to Africa. Included in the ranks of this group are the waxbills, the mannikins, the munias, and the beautiful Grass Finches of Australia. The asking price for these species will range from the least expensive of any finches to quite large sums for those such as the Crimson Finch of Australia. Color mutations of Australian finches will command even higher prices depending on the species and the mutation.

Many are reliable breeders and of course

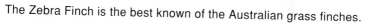

The Zebra Finch is the best known of the Australian grass finches.

Crested Fawn-and-White Bengalese Finch.

the Zebra Finch is so prolific that it is regarded as domesticated in most countries—as is the Bengalese or Society Finch. Members of this family have a number of characteristics in common. The nests are domed, the eggs are white and unmarked and the young, which are reared by both parents, do not solicit food in a normal gape manner but twist their heads round while in a crouched position.

Most are good

The Zebra Finch derives its name from the black-and-white striping on the throat and breast of the male.

mixers in a communal aviary, providing consideration is given to their size, or rather, in many cases, their lack of it. Certain species are quite hardy but it is perhaps always better to qualify this by saying that even so-called hardy species would not survive harsh winters. In these areas, a minimum of an enclosed shelter is recommended and in many instances a degree of heat during the coldest months is advised. Likewise, extended daylight hours via artificial lighting will more equate the longer daylight of the bird's natural environment.

Waxbills

All but three species of these delightful little birds are native to Africa. Most are very modest in price, being

Fawn-and-White Bengalese Finch.

The pied trait has appeared in both Bengalese and Zebra finches, as in the Fawn-and-White Bengalese Finch (facing page) and a Pied Zebra Finch hen (above).

exported in large numbers each year. Although a few are vividly colored, many are not, though all have color in their plumage, and are attractive. The majority have red wax-colored beaks—their name referring to the similarity to the red wax used of old for sealing documents. They form lasting pairs and seem to exhibit very strong attachment for their mates. They are active little birds and I have never found them in any way aggressive in mixed company; quite the opposite—it is they that need protection from larger finch species, most of which should not be housed with them. Strangely enough, they are quite safe with certain much larger non-finch strong

A trio of Zebra Finches; the hen exhibits dilution in plumage color.

A cock Zebra Finch in flight.

attachment for their birds such as Diamond Doves and even Cockatiels—the latter being about the most gentle bird I know in mixed company.

When breeding, the cocks usually display by parading around with a piece of dried grass or something similar and this can be most amusing when the hen shows no interest and flies off to leave her mate wondering if the stalk was the right one, so he goes in search of a more "attractive" offering to induce his partner to commence breeding. The feeding requirements are as discussed in the

With domestication, the markings in Zebra Finches can be quite variable in extent.

Although undemanding with respect to accommodations, Zebra Finches will enjoy a planted enclosure.

chapter on feeding with due consideration for the small size of these birds, so that the smaller seeds will be preferred, along with greenfood and livefood. Grass heads and similar food should be securely fixed for the small species which, in effect, tear the greens so need them firmly anchored to achieve this.

Pied Hen Zebra Finch. In this variety, pigment is missing from various areas of the plumage.

Zebra Finch cock showing the full range of colors present in the wild forms of this species.

Rear view of a Chestnut-flanked White Zebra Finch cock. In this variety, the dilution of coloration is quite variable.

Front view of the Chestnut-flanked White Zebra Finch shown on the facing page.

I have listed herewith a number of the more readily available species and described two further examples which are typical of this group.

SOME POPULAR WAXBILLS

Aurora Finch (Crimson-winged Pytilia)

Pytilia phoenicoptera
12cm (4 1/2 in.)

Gray, with red in wings and dark gray beak. Pytilias are hosts to various parasitic whydahs whose chicks they rear alongside their own. Occasionally available, middle price range.

In the Black-cheeked Waxbill, *Estrilda erythronotos*, the sexes are very difficult to distinguish.

Senegal Fire Finch, *Lagonosticta senegala,* male and female.

Peter's Twinspot
Hypargos niveoguttatus
12cm (4 1/2 in.)

Vivid red over black underparts with white side spots. Beak steel blue/black. Very attractive. Occasionally available, middle price range. Delicate.

Melba Finch (Greenwinged Pytilia)
Pytilia melba 13cm (5 in.)

Red forehead and throat, yellow chest, red tail, wings green with white underparts barred with black. Very attractive. Occasionally available, middle price range. Delicate.

Most fanciers would agree that the Melba Finch, *Pytilia melba*, is the most attractively colored of the *Pytilia* finches.

Senegal Fire Finch

Lagonosticta senegala
10cm (4 in.)

Somewhat dull, mainly brown with red underparts. Common, low price.

Violet-eared Waxbill

Uraeginthus granatina
13cm (5 in.)

Forehead blue, throat black, cheeks violet, body rich brown, rump blue and beak red.

Very desirable but delicate. Mid to high price, reasonable availability. Similar but with more blue is the Purple Grenadier, *U. ianthinogaster.*

Lavender Finch
Estrilda caerulescens
12cm (4 1/2 in.)
  Blue-gray with red

Right and below: The Orange-cheeked Waxbill, *Estrilda melpoda,* shown perched and in flight, is easy to care for and will not trouble other species housed with it.

Above: The Gold-breasted Waxbill, *Amandava subflava*, is the smallest of the estrildid finches.

tail feathers, beak black and red. Very popular and usually available, modest price.

Orange-cheeked Waxbill
Estrilda melpoda
10cm (4 in.)

Basically gray and brown with orange cheeks and whitish throat and rump. Beak red. Very popular and

Right: The striping on the underparts of the Common Waxbill, *Estrilda astrild*, is just visible here.

View of a Red-eared Waxbill, *Estrilda troglodytes*, in flight. This little finch will prove a problem-free aviary subject.

low priced attractive bird. Other low priced waxbills similar to this species are the Red-eared Waxbill (Black-rumped) *E.troglodytes*, and the St. Helena Waxbill (Common Waxbill), *E. astrild*. The more attractive Blackcheeked Waxbill, *E. erythronotos*, with its red underparts and hints of pink in the shoulders will cost you somewhat more when available.

Cordon Bleus
Uraeginthus
13cm (5 in.)

There are three species of the Cordon Bleu and each is most appealing. They are highly recommended for those just entering the hobby and are usually reliable breeders. They are also very peaceful birds and are better for being housed with similar birds. This is especially true when breeding and even very friendly species like Zebra Finches (overfriendly?) have been known to upset the breeding of these birds. Although they are sometimes described as hardy, I would not chance my birds in a harsh winter, where I think some heat, albeit low output, must be available in the worst months. Even if the birds survived low temperatures I wonder to what extent it

Red-cheeked Cordon Bleu, *Uraeginthus bengalus,* male and female.

The male Red-cheeked Cordon Bleu is easily distinguished; whether the other bird is a female or an individual of the species *angolensis* is not apparent.

affects future breeding performance and longevity—which in this species is normally quite good.

Being a quiet bird they prefer planted aviaries where they will nest in wicker nesting baskets, or they will build their own if sufficient material and cover is available. The species are identified as follows: Red-cheeked Cordon Bleu, U.bengalus has blue underparts with brown above and the cock sports red cheek patches these are missing in the hen. The Blue-breasted, U. angolensis is similar to the Redcheek hen but the blue is somewhat paler. The Bluecapped, U. *cyanocephala*, has no cheek spots and the blue extends over the head; females are similar but with much reduced area of blue and little, if any, on the head.

Distribution West, central, east and southern Africa.

Blue-breasted Cordon Bleus, *Uraeginthus angolensis*, bathing in a puddle in Kruger National Park in Africa.

The Blue-capped Cordon Bleu, *Uraeginthus cyanocephala*, a male.

All three Cordon Bleu species—this is a male Blue-capped, *Uraeginthus cyanocephala*—are similarly undemanding in their requirements.

Breeding Four to six eggs incubated by both parents over 12 to 14 days. Fledging 14 to 16 days and independent after a further 10 to 12 days. These species are not aggressive to conspecifics when breeding.

Gold-breasted Waxbill (Zebra Waxbill) *Amandava subflava* 9cm (3 1/2 in.)

Also known as the Orange-breasted Waxbill, this little bird is the smallest finch you can buy—and a delightful choice it would be. It is

Above: A male Red Avadavat, *Amandava amandava*, in full color (nuptial plumage).

reasonably inexpensive—about the same price as the Cordon Bleus and is a good value. It is friendly, active and a reliable breeder; it is also very colorful so has a lot going for it. The beak is red and there is a red stripe above the eyes; back and wings are gray-green and the underbody orange with

Right: The Green Avadavat, *Amandava formosa*, is native to India.

A Red Avadavat pair. The much plainer females have sometimes been dyed with food colorings to make them more appealing to potential buyers.

yellow—the latter barred with gray. They are quite happy in a mixed aviary with other waxbills and will tolerate their own kind when breeding. Plenty of cover will reduce minor squabbling. They will also breed both in indoor flights and cages but the latter is not advised.

Distribution Senegal, Ethiopia and Uganda.

Hen Duller version of the cock and with no red stripe over eyes.

Breeding Wicker basket in dense cover; reasonably low down. Clutch is three to five, incubated by both parents in 12 to 14 days. Fledging at 17 to

Male Red Avadavat. The subspecies exhibit different shades of the reddish tone from which they take their name.

Above and opposite, below: The Green Avadavat, *Amandava formosa*, is indeed greenish—the differences in appearance here no doubt derive from the ambient lighting.

Opposite, above: One of the subspecies of the Chestnut Munia, *Lonchura malacca*, is also known as the Tricolored Nun.

Of the forms of the Chestnut Munia, *Lonchura malacca*, some are frequently available to bird keepers.

Zebra Finch varieties: (1) Dilute Fawn; (2) Silver; (3) Normal; (4) Fawn; (5) White.

Chestnut-flanked White Zebra Finch.

avadavats. The Red Munia, *A.amandava*, also known as the Strawberry or Tiger Finch, is much more readily available, and cheaper, than the prettier Green Munia or Avadavat, *A.formosa*. The Red Munia is the better initial choice for a beginner, being the easier to breed.

AUSTRALIAN FINCHES

There are 20 species of finches found in Australia, of which two, the Nutmeg Mannikin and the Black-headed Nun (Chestnut Mannikin) have been introduced. There are many who would say that one species, the Gouldian Finch, is the most beautiful finch in the world, and certainly once seen it is never forgotten.

21 days and youngsters may safely be left with the parents.

Goldbreasts are relatives of two other popular aviary birds, but which are native to India, known as

As a group, Australian finches are always expensive, with the exception of the Zebra Finch—which is

Zebra finch varieties: top, pied fawn; lower two birds, pied gray pair, with male at bottom.

Cock Zebra Finch of the
Black-breasted variety.

usual requirements
when breeding are for
wicker nesting baskets
though many will
accept half-open
nestboxes, or funnels
in which nesting
material (grasses, etc.)
has been placed. Most
will also nest in thickly
planted aviaries. Being
birds of the grasslands
they should be
supplied with as much
of this as possible.
Panicum and canary
seeds are favorite, with
other seed added for
variety. Chickweed is a
favored greenfood, but
a range of wild plants
should be offered and
notes kept on those
accepted. The amount
of insectivorous food
taken will vary,
Gouldians possibly
being the species which
will most readily take
this in any quantity.

so well established in
captivity that it is
probably the most
inexpensive finch you
could purchase.

The care in the aviary
is the same for this
group of birds as for
other finches, and the

In general, other
than the Zebra Finch,
the newcomer to this
hobby is not advised to
commence by including

Zebra Finch varieties: (1) Pied Fawn; (2) Pied Silver; (3) Silver.

Pied Zebra Finch cock.

Australian finches in a collection until experience has been gained with less expensive birds. Acclimatization is very important to these birds if they are cage-bred and are to be released into aviaries. They cannot stand damp conditions that are also cold. This even applies to Australians, who should retain them indoors over the first winter if they live in the colder states.

There are a number of color mutations found in the Gouldian and other Australian Finches and these have an enthusiastic specialist following—prices will be very expensive in most cases—those in the Zebra Finch again being the exception. If you are interested in Australia's finches then you are strongly recommended to join one of the specialist

Although many varieties of Zebra Finches exist, locating particular ones, like this Fawn Penguin, often proves difficult.

The red-headed morph of the Gouldian Finch, in which the face of the
female shows considerable black.

Male Gouldian Finch the black-headed form.

AUSTRALIAN FINCH SPECIES

Sydney Waxbill (Red-browed) Firetail	*Aegintha temporalis*	10 cm. (4 in.)
Painted Finch	*Emblema picta*	11 cm. (4.25 in.)
Beautiful Firetail	*Emblema bella*	12 cm. (4.75 in.)
Red-eared Firetail	*Emblema oculata*	12 cm. (4.75 in.)
Diamond Firetail	*Emblema guttata*	12 cm. (4.75 in.)
Crimson Finch	*Neochmia phaeton*	14 cm. (5.50 in.)
Star Finch	*Neochmia ruficauda*	12 cm. (4.75 in.)
Zebra Finch (Spotted -sided)	*Poephila guttata*	10cm. (4in.)
Bicheno Finch (Double-barred)	*Poephila bichenovii*	11 cm. (4.25 in.)
Masked Finch	*Poephila personata*	12 cm (4.75 in.)
Long-tailed Finch	*Poephila acuticauda*	15 cm. (5.75 in.)
Parson Finch (Black-throated finch)	*Poephila cincta*	10 cm. (4 in.)
Blue-faced Parrot Finch	*Erythrura trichroa*	12cm. (4.75 in.)
Gouldian Finch	*Chloebia gouldiae*	14 cm. (5.50 in.)
Plum-headed Finch	*Aidemosyne modesta*	
Nutmeg Mannikin (Introduced species)	*Lonchura punctulata*	11 cm. (4.25 in.)
Blackheaded Nun (Munia)	*Lonchura malacca*	11 cm. (4.25 in.)
Yellow-rumped Mannikin (Yellow-tailed)	*Lonchura flaviprymna*	10 cm. (4 in.)
Chestnut-breasted Mannikin	*Lonchura castaneothorax*	10 cm. (4 in.)
Pictorella Finch	*Lonchura pictoralis*	11 cm. (4.25 in.)

This view of a Zebra Finch in flight illustrates the interplay between the wing feathers and the air.

Fawn Zebra Finch cock, a yellow-beaked variant.

societies of these birds who do a really excellent job of keeping members informed on all aspects of the various species.

Mannikins and Munias

This group of birds comprises only about 17 species which are found in aviculture in any sort of numbers; of these about eight to ten are very popular and available at modest prices. They are not especially colorful birds, the gray, black, and white of the Java Sparrow being the most striking member; most are combinations of dark and light brown

Java Sparrow, *Padda oryzivora*.

Pied variety of the Java Sparrow, *Padda oryzivora.*

with black and white featuring in the various species. However, their popularity in aviaries is because they are very social with their own kind, they are very hardy once acclimatized, they subsist on an all-seed diet better than many finches, and they always seem to look quite immaculate in their plumage. Further, they are all tough little birds and can safely be kept with birds such as weavers and others who try to bully aviary companions.

Of course, the most famous member is probably the Bengalese, which was developed from the White-backed Munia. This domesticated variety is known as the Society Finch, which is very apt—indeed, a name such as "the friendly finch" would not be out of place with this species. Bates and Busenbark in *Finches & Softbilled Birds* describe them admirably, "The only real problem with the Society Finch is that it is friendly and helpful to a meddlesome degree. When a Society sees another bird preparing a nest, it just naturally wants to assist. When the nest is finished, the Society will help incubate the eggs." You cannot get any more friendly than that! The authors go on to say that they have had Society Birds swap, on a day to day basis, with equally friendly Zebra Finches, the incubation of each other's broods. Bengalese are in fact much used as foster parents to Gouldian Finches and numerous other species. Bengalese are four and three-quarter inches in length, and are available in a number of color forms—all a variation of white and brown.

All but two of this group of birds do not show sexual variation, but this is easily overcome by placing a few "pairs" in an aviary containing ample nestboxes or wicker baskets (both is better) and the birds will soon pair off and settle down to breed. The range of distribution in the various species is Africa, Asia, through many Pacific Islands, and extends to northern Australia in three species.

Munias of the species *Lonchura malacca* are always popular and include the Black-headed Nun (Chestnut Mannikin), *L.*

Zebra Finch, eight days old. In estrildid finches, the mouth markings of nestlings are species-characteristic.

Fawn-and-White Bengalese Finches.

m. atricapilla, a bird of four and one-quarter inches; this bird has a black hood with brown lower body set off by a light gray beak. The Tricolored Nun is similar but has white down its chest and abdomen, thus looking somewhat brighter. The third popular nun is the White-Headed nun (Pale-headed Mannikin), *L. maja*, which has a white hood.

Black-headed Nun, *Lonchura malacca atricapilla.*

Tri-colored Nun, *Lonchura malacca malacca.*

Left: Chestnut-and White Bengalese Finches.

Right: Bengalese Finches, Dilute Fawn.

Left: Bengalese Finches, Self Chestnut.

White-headed Nuns, *Lonchura maja.*

Cutthroat Finch, *Amadina fasciata.*

In contrast to the more sombre colors of the nuns is the Java Sparrow, *Padda oryzivora*, with its gray body, black head, and white cheek patches.

Javas are best bred in small groups of their own kind, but also make nice additions to a mixed aviary—where they need to be with species able to stand

Cutthroat Finch, a male—the female lacks the bright throat band.

Above and opposite page:
Red-headed Finches, *Amadina erythrocephala:* juvenile (above) and adult (facing page).

up to these tough little birds of up to five and one-half inches. There are white and cinnamon mutations but these will cost somewhat more. A large-sized budgie-nestbox will suit these birds.

The two members of the genus *Amadina* are very well-known to birdkeepers. One is the Cutthroat *A.fasciata*, a mottled bird with a bright red flash around its throat; the female lacks this. These are hardy birds and safe in a mixed collection, but not when breeding as they are very aggressive, so in mixed company need to be with birds of similar nature. The Red-headed Finch (Paradise Sparrow), *A.erythrocephala* is far less imported but is, I feel, a prettier bird than the Cutthroat, though on the same lines. Again, it will not

Indian Silverbill, *Lonchura malabarica*.

think anything of taking another bird's nesting material, so at breeding times place it with those that will not allow this.

The last birds I will mention in this family are the African and Indian Silverbills, *Lonchura cantans* and *L.malabarica*. These are friendly little birds that are quite safe with smaller finches and are ready breeders, both in

African Silverbill, *Lonchura cantans*.

aviaries and cages. They are rather plain to look at, mixtures of brown and white, but they have a lot of character and, like Bengalese, are sometimes used as foster parents. Their willingness to tolerate other birds is shown by the fact that two (or more) hens have been known to use the same nest—which can mean a lot of eggs to incubate; in such circumstances the eggs should be spread among other nests. Silverbills are very modestly priced and it will probably be the African species you will be buying.

FAMILY PLOCEIDAE

This family of finchlike birds is divided into four subfamilies which, between them, contain 158 species in 22 genera. It is an interesting group from an avicultural viewpoint because its members represent many challenges to breeders. For example, the whydahs of the genus *Vidua* (subfamily Viduinae) are parasitic on various small finch species when breeding. The weavers are often polygamous and the nonparasitic whydahs, though easy to maintain, have rarely been bred.

Many species in this family have nuptial plumage—by which is meant that during the breeding season the males grow vividly colored feathers, or long tails, which changes them from drab sparrowlike birds to gems of the avian world. Only the males show this plumage change and in their non-breeding feather they are said to be in eclipse plumage.

The singular problem with many birds in this

Male House Sparrow, *Passer domesticus*. This bird is a familiar sight in most cities of the world, thanks to its adaptability to civilization.

family is that there are always more cocks on sale than hens. This is because even if trapped during the breeding season, when sexes are obvious, among the "hens" will be found many immature cocks since it takes them two seasons to molt into full plumage; further, as cocks are bolder than hens, more of them tend to be caught. It is thus more difficult to purchase breeding pairs or trios.

One species in the family is known to everyone, and that is the Common House Sparrow, *Passer domesticus*, which was

Albinism occurs regularly among wild House Sparrows, and the trait is cultivated in captive stocks.

Female House Sparrow, the paradigm for the "sparrow-like bird."

Pin-tailed Whydah, *Vidua macroura*.

originally native to Africa and Europe, but has been introduced to most countries, including the U.S.A. and Australia, where it has quickly established itself as a native bird.

Subfamily Viduinae

There are 10 members in this subfamily, four being called indigo birds and the others being known as whydahs. All are brood parasites on finches, though our knowledge of the group is far from complete, and it may well be that more than one species is able to build a nest and rear its own young—being parasitic when the opportunity arises. Unlike cuckoos, who remove the eggs of the host, whydahs do not, the host rearing both their own chicks and those of the whydah. For this to be possible the whydahs have evolved in such a way that their young closely resemble the chicks of the host at all stages, from the eggs to the fledgling. Because of this need for specific host finches, breeding whydahs is extremely difficult and the beginner is not advised to attempt this until experience is gained with other finch species. Nonetheless, one or two whydahs are popular in mixed collections, and available at reasonable prices.

Pin-tailed Whydahs, male and female. The sparrow-like whydah hens are not very distinctively marked, nor do they change plumage as the males do.

The most common is usually the Pintailed Whydah, *Vidua macroura*, which has a body length in eclipse plumage of four inches; in full nuptial plumage the long tail feathers increase the length to 11 inches and at this time the cocks are most impressive in their black and white feathering. In spite of their small size, these can be aggressive birds when in breeding feather, so need to be placed with other weavers or finches such as Java Sparrows, Cutthroats and those mentioned previously which can match the Pintail in the aggression stakes! Because of their bullying tactics with small finches, breeding is even less likely, as they are likely to intimidate even their hosts in small confines. A very large aviary would be needed to breed them, when St. Helena Waxbills, Fire Finches, and other possible hosts (the Pintail is unusual in using more than one host species), could be placed with a pair and such that they could escape the Pintail if

Red-eared Waxbills are thought to be parasitized by the Pin-tailed Whydah.

required.

Another popular whydah is the Paradise, V. paradisaea, which in nuptial feather is black and fawn, with magnificent tail feathers displaying a latticelike pattern on them. This is somewhat larger than the Pintail Whydah, and the tail feathers are broader. It is also far less aggressive in a mixed collection and normally is parasitic on the Melba Finch, though abnormal hosts have been used with success, e.g., the African Firefinch.

Other whydahs sometimes available will include the Queen Whydah (Shaft-tailed), *V. regia* and the Fischer's Whydah, *V.fischeri.* The indigo birds are also known as Combassous, and are similar to whydahs only not possessing the long tail feathers.

Fischer's Whydah, *Vidua fischeri.*

Both whydahs and indigo birds are of African distribution and will happily live on a mixed finch diet to which livefood and greenfood should be added. They are hardy once acclimatized and long-lived (up to 20 years). Obviously, in order to fully appreciate their beautiful flight they are best suited to very large aviaries which include high perches in order that their tail feathers are not at risk of being unduly damaged.

Subfamily Passerinae

This group is comprised of the sparrows and the one you are most likely to find in your pet shop will be the Sudan Golden Sparrow, *Auripasser luteus*, of North Africa. This is largely a yellow bird of five inches. In the hen, the chest is more of a gray. They are hardy birds and can be purchased at a modest price—about the same as that for Gray Singing Finches or Java Sparrows. Once acclimatized they will live happily in unheated accommodation, but should not be housed with smaller finches as they are quite aggressive birds, though safe with those such as weavers, Javas and others able to give as well as take. Although one could try to breed with a single pair, much better results are likely if a few pairs are kept as a small colony when they should be provided with plenty of thick nesting cover—privet, gorse, etc. They will use virtually anything as nest material, and nestboxes of various types can be supplied as they are cosmopolitan in their choice. Normally, a standard finch mix with a good percentage of canary seed in it will suffice, but when breeding, greenfood and livefood is needed in goodly quantities.

Two nice little birds in a related genus to

The nests constructed of interwoven grasses are the basis for calling the birds "weavers."

the sparrows are the Scaly Weaver, *Sporopipes squamifrons*, four inches, and the Speckle-fronted Weaver, *S.frontalis*, and a half inches. The former are quietly colored in black, white, and gray with a mottled head pattern. They have the advantage that the colors are "year 'round" in both sexes, which look alike, thus making it difficult to obtain true pairs. They are very peaceful little birds and will even be safe with waxbills, though it is advisable to keep them with slightly larger species come the breeding season when they can become more assertive. The Speckle-front has white underparts, sparrow-colored wings and a chestnut neck. The white cheeks are highlighted by a small black mustache. This species is similar in behavior to the scalycrowns, and both species should be acclimatized with great care, and provided with mildly heated quarters during the winter months. Prices are quite reasonable when the birds are available and they are well recommended.

Subfamily Ploceinae

This subfamily contains most of the popular members of the family including the extremely popular "bishops." Nearly all members of the group exhibit nuptial plumage and build the complex nest mentioned earlier in the text. They are not suited to cagelife, and are better kept in small groups in an aviary. As they are very confident birds, they should be kept only with similar birds in a mixed aviary; otherwise they will bully smaller or more

The Golden Sparrow, *Auripasser luteus*, is one of the most familiar weavers.

Green Singing Finch,
Serinus mozambicus.

docile species. Many have been successfully bred, but two factors have restricted this, namely their low cost and the difficulty in obtaining hens. This is compounded by the fact that they are invariably bought as pairs, whereas if a small colony, say ten birds or more, were purchased, and given their own aviary, this would greatly improve the chances of successful breeding. The sight of a number of cocks in full color phase is most attractive in a well-planted environment. Weavers, which comprise most of this subfamily, can be somewhat hard on plantings, compared to most finches, but if hardy varieties, like gorse, are included, this will reduce this tendency, beyond which one should try to supply a whole range of nesting materials which will again distract them somewhat from the bushes. By attempting colony breeding one obviously improves the chances of having at least a couple of hens within the group; if all non-males are ringed with plastic rings, then it should be possible for you to build a very clear picture of the sexes as any immatures that color up later can thus be banded accordingly, males being given a different color ring so they can be identified out of breeding season.

The largest genus in this subfamily is Ploceus, and all but four species are of African distribution. Yellow features strongly in the plumage of the cocks and this is contrasted with black and, very often, orange. There

are, however, some species which have no yellow in the plumage, for example Vieillot's Black Weaver, *P.nigerrimus*, though these are rarely, if ever available—though one can never tell what the future holds.

An attractive small weaver is the Little Masked, *P.luteolus*, which is four and a half inches in length. It has a black facial area, well defined from the yellow of the body; the wings are black, edged with yellow. The female is a very duller version altogether. As weavers go, this is a peaceful little bird that nests in thorn trees and often in single pairs or very small colonies. The eggs are white and two or three are laid. A very similar bird is the Slenderbilled Weaver, *P.pelzelni.*

More readily available will be the

larger "Yellow" Weavers, but as these are much larger—a minimum of six inches or more—they cannot be kept with any of the finches described in this book, as they are far too aggressive. However, in a mixed aviary containing such birds as budgerigars or cardinals and similar-sized avians, they would be quite safe. An aviary devoted to these larger weavers would be most attractive. Those most likely to be available will be:

impossible—when the males are in eclipse plumage.

Similar in size, seven inches, to the larger yellow weavers are those of the genus *Malimbus*. These birds are predominantly red and black and one, the Crested Malimbe, *M.malimbicus*, is the only weaver to sport a crest. Their care is the same as for other large weavers in that they require a highly insectivorous diet. Being large birds, they are quite bold and thus can becom very tame in

Vitelline or Halfmasked (African Masked), *P. velatus*

Village weaver, *P. cucuilatus*

Black-headed weaver, *P. melanocephalus*

There are, in fact, many species, and distinguishing between them can be very difficult—almost much the same manner as many softbilled birds. You would be fortunate indeed to see a malimbe for sale but

The Red-billed Quelea, *Quela quelea*, is the most numerous weaver species and is frequently destroyed as a pest.

The Red-headed Quelea, *Quelea erythrops*, is native to southern Africa.

Red-headed and Redbilled Queleas, *Quelea erythrops* and *Q.quelea*. They are rather plain birds, but are quite safe in mixed aviaries with other finches. The latter variety are very industrious birds and will begin nestbuilding almost as soon as they enter an aviary. Very soon you will have a beautifully domed nest on view but alas they usually dismantle this in order to build another! Little data is available on their breeding but they are hardy birds once acclimatized and make excellent birds for beginners. Supply plenty of grasses for nest activities, or they will be seen plucking feathers from other birds in the aviary.

I mention them simply because they are attractive and may one day be seen on lists. Two very inexpensive weavers that are usually for sale are the

THE BISHOPS

There are three or four birds of the genus *Euplectes* which are both very popular and available, these being known as Bishops due to the mantles of color—red or yellow—that adorn the males when in nuptial plumage. In eclipse plumage, you would never believe these males were the same species as they become dowdy and sparrowlike, just like the hens.

They are very modestly priced (unless you live in Australia where they are extremely rare and expensive), and are quite safe in aviaries containing the larger and robust finches such as Cutthroats, Java Sparrows as well as other similar sized weavers. In length they are all about four and a half inches. Bishops are polygamous, so when attempting to breed, two or three hens should be placed with

The Napoleon Weaver, *Euplectes afer*, a male.

a male. Ideally, they should be bred in small colonies in very well-planted aviaries.

The Napoleon Weaver (Golden Bishop), *E. afer*, is a

Bright and contrasting coloration accounts for the popularity of weaver birds such as the Napoleon, *Euplectes afer*.

mixture of vivid yellow and black on the body and head, with dark brown in the wings. Hen is sparrowlike in colors. A feature of these birds, and other Bishops, is the male's habit of leaping into the air during his courting display. Males defend their territories very strongly against other birds, especially their own kind, thus a spacious aviary is recommended. Their nests are commenced by the cock, and completed by the hen who will lay and incubate two to four grayish-white, speckled eggs. There are four subspecies of which the Taha Bishop, *E.a.taha*, is the best known, though not as striking as the nominate race.

The very popular Red Bishop, *E.orix*, with its bright, crimson-red cape and

Some forms of *Euplectes orix* are more orange; this is the nominate subspecies.

chest, black body and head with brown wings, is a most impressive bird. There are four subspecies and Orange Bishops occur in the wild state, where orange replaces the red plumage. It is sometimes said that the Orange Bishop is actually a "faded" red, seen when birds have molted out in captivity, but this is not so, though most Bishops do fade in captivity; this is probably due to a dietary deficiency which affects the color density. The Orange Bishop is the subspecies *E.o.franciscana*. The Red Bishop is also known as the Grenadier Weaver. An aviary containing both Red and Orange Bishops makes a striking contrast but the aviary should be large.

Red Bishops lay two

The Crimson-crowned Weaver, *Euplectes hordaceus,* resembles the Red Bishop.

Bishops: a hen between two males of the subspecies *Euplectes orix franciscana*.

to four deep blue eggs which are incubated by the hen for 12 days and the chicks fledge some 14 days after this. In all cases, the young of Bishops are fed by the hen, while the cock devotes his time to guarding the nest(s). If attempting to breed Bishops be prepared for many failures, but that will make success all the more pleasing. It is essential that plenty of varied livefood is available constantly throughout the breeding season.

NON PARASITIC WHYDAHS

Closely related to the bishops, and in the same genus, are seven species of whydah which are not brood parasites. It was for a long while thought that these whydahs were polygamous but it is now thought that at least a few of them are, in fact, monogamous. The courting displays are always interesting affairs, combining hovering and little dances on the ground. The major feature of whydahs in nuptial plumage is, of course, their magnificent tail feathers which grow very long. Black is the predominant color and this is contrasted by various amounts of red, yellow, brown, or tan, according to the species.

Whydahs are at their best in large, planted

Despite differences in appearance, whydahs such as the Fan-tailed, *Euplectes axillaris*, are closely related to the bishops.

Above: The Red-collared Whydah, *Euplectes ardens,* has a wide distribution throughout Africa south of the Sahara.

aviaries though species such as the Jackson's, sad to say, will strip this bare, though not if it has numerous conifers in it. None have any reliable record of being good breeders, but as they are usually very hardy birds, once well acclimatized, they are thus excellent birds to adorn even a beginner's aviary. They require only a simple finch mix diet, plus a supply of greenfood and livefood. Few are readily available and are usually somewhat expensive as a result.

Possibly the most desirable is Jackson's *Euplectes jacksoni,* which is a very showy bird and many regard as the most intelligent of the whydahs. In breeding plumage it is glossy black and has a total length of 12 inches. More readily available, and less expensive, will be the

The Yellow-rumped Bishop, *Euplectes capensis,* comprises several subspecies.

Yellow-mantled Whydah, *Euplectes macrourus*, a cock in nuptial plumage.

Redcollared Whydah, *E. ardens*, a bird attaining 14 inches in length with its very long tail. Even larger is the Giant Whydah (Long-tailed), *E.progne*, which may have a total length of 22 inches, of which about 16 inches is composed of the beautiful tail feathers. Breeding of all of these whydahs is unlikely, but tall grasses would seem to be important, as these would be found in their natural habitat and rushes found near water courses. In mixed aviaries they should be placed with species of similar body size.

Some of the possible variations in coloration can be seen in this group of *Euplectes* weavers, apparently the species *orix* and *hordaceus*.

Index

Acanthis cannabina, 146
Acclimatization, 49
African Silverbill, 35, 225
Airsac mite, 107
Alexander the Great, 7
Amadina erythrocephala, 222
Amadina fasciata, 34, 220
Amandava amandava, 193
Amandava formosa, 193
Amandava subflava, 123, 186
American Goldfinch, 158
Auripasser luteus, 236
Aurora Finch, 182
Aviaries, 15
Baya Weaver, 114
Birdrooms, 34
Blackcrested Finch, 128
Black-tailed Lavender Waxbill, 92
Blue-capped Cordon Bleu, 191
Brambling, 145
Budgerigars, 8
Cages, 35
Cardinalis cardinalis, 124
Carduelis cucullata, 156
Carduelis spinoides, 65
Carpodacus mexicanus, 127, 165
Chaffinch, 143
Chestnut-breasted Mannikin, 41
Chloebia gouldiae, 48
Coccothraustes personatus, 63, 63

Common Waxbill, 186
Crimson-crowned Weaver, 246
Crop milk, 95
Cuban Finch, 132
Cutthroat Finch, 34, 220
Dark Firefinch, 93
Diamond Firetail, 49
Diarrhea, 109
Diet, 54
Duke de Nivernais, 7
Duke of Bedford, 52
Eggbinding, 109
Egglaying, 94
Emblema guttata, 49
Erythrina erythrina, 162
Erythrura prasina, 61
Estrilda astrild, 186
Estrilda caerulescens, 184
Estrilda melpoda, 185
Estrilda perreini, 92
Estrilda troglodytes, 121, 187
Euplectes afer, 243
Euplectes ardens, 250
Euplectes capensis, 250
Euplectes hordaceus, 246
Euplectes macrourus, 252
Eurasian Bullfinch, 148
Eurasian Linnet, 146
European Bullfinch, 120
European Goldfinch, 157
Feather plucking, 110
Fischer's Whydah, 233
Fledging, 96
Fostering, 100

Foudia madagascariensis, 107
Fringilla coelebs, 143
Fringilla montifringilla, 145
Gold-breasted Waxbill, 123, 186, 190
Golden Sparrow, 236
Gouldian Finch, 48, 207
Gray Singing Finch, 106
Green Avadavat, 193, 196
Greenfoods, 61
Green Twinspot, 101
Grit, 68
Hand-rearing, 102
Himalayan Greenfinch, 65
Hooded Siskin, 156
House Finch, 127, 165
House Sparrow, 227
Hypargos niveoguttatus, 183
Indian Silverbill, 225
Indigo Bunting, 138
Insectivorous foods, 68
Ionizer, 35
Jacarini Finch, 59
Jamrach, Christian, 9
Java Sparrow, 42, 211
Lagonosticta rubricata, 93
Lagonosticta senegala, 184
Lavender Finch, 184
Lazuli Bunting, 138
Linnaeus, Carolus, 118
Livefood, 64
Lonchura cantans, 35, 225
Lonchura castaneothorax, 41
Lonchura maja, 219
Lonchura malabarica, 225
Lonchura malacca, 196
Lophospingus pusillus, 128
Macaws, 8
Madagascar Weaver, 107
Mandingoa nitidula, 101

Masked Hawfinch, 63
Melba Finch, 183
Minerals, 68
Napoleon Weaver, 243
Neochmia ruficauda, 68
Nestboxes, 84
New World Buntings, 135
Olive Finch, 135
Orange-breasted Bunting, 137
Orange-cheeked Waxbill, 185
Overcrowding, 104
Owl Finch, 62
Padda orzivora, 42, 211
Painted Bunting, 138
Parasites, 112
Parrot-billed Seedeater, 43
Passer domesticus, 227, 228
Passerina amoena, 139
Passerina cyanea, 138
Passerina leclancheri, 137
Passerina versicolor, 139
Peter's Twinspot, 183
Pintailed Parrot Finch, 61
Pin-tailed Whydah, 230
Ploceus phillipinus, 114
Poephila bichenovii, 62
Poephila guttata, 27
Purple Grenadier Waxbill, 44
Pyrrhula pyrrhula, 120
Pytilia melba, 183
Pytilia phoenicoptera, 182
Quelea erythrops, 242
Quelea quelea, 241
Red Avadavat, 193
Red-billed Firefinch, 51
Red-billed Quelea, 241
Red-cheeked Cordon Bleu, 108, 189
Red-collared Whydah, 250
Red-cowled Cardinal, 12

Red-eared Waxbill, 121, 187
Red-headed Finches, 222
Red-headed Quelea, 242
Saffron Finch, 128
Scalyface, 114
Scalyleg, 114
Scaly Weaver, 234
Scarlet Rosefinch, 162
Seed, 57
Seed hopper, 31
Senegal Fire Finch, 184
Serinus atrogularis, 126
Serinus leucopygius, 55
Show cages, 39
Sicalis flaveola, 128
Sporophila albogularis, 55
Sporophila peruviana, 43
Sporopipes squamifrons, 234
Star Finch, 68
Tiaris canora, 132
Tiaris olivacea, 135
Tricolored Nun, 196, 216
Trollope, Jeffrey, 52

Uraeginthus bengalus, 108, 189
Uraeginthus cyanocephala, 191
Uraeginthus granatina, 109, 184
Uraeginthus ianthinogaster, 44, 95
Versicolor Bunting, 138
Vidua fischeri, 233
Vidua macroura, 230
Violet-eared Waxbill, 109, 184
Virginia Cardinal, 124
Volatinia jacarina, 59
White-headed Nun, 219
White-throated Seedeater, 55
Yellow-mantled Whydah, 252
Yellow-rumped Bishop, 250
Yellow-rumped Seedeater, 126
Zebra Finch, 44, 169, 171, 175, 209